The Harcourt Brace Casebook Series in Literature

"The Yellow Wallpaper"

Charlotte Perkins Gilman

The Harcourt Brace Casebook Series in Literature
Series Editors: Laurie G. Kirszner and Stephen R. Mandell

"The Yellow Wallpaper"

Charlotte Perkins Gilman

Contributing Editor

Carol Kivo
Pepperdine University

Harcourt Brace College Publishers

Fort Worth   Philadelphia   San Diego   New York   Orlando   Austin   San Antonio
Toronto   Montreal   London   Sydney   Tokyo

Publisher:	Earl McPeek
Acquisitions Editor:	Julie McBurney
Developmental Editor:	Katie Frushour
Project Editor:	Andrea Wright
Art Director:	Vicki Whistler
Production Manager:	Linda McMillan

ISBN: 0-15-505485-6
Library of Congress Catalog Card Number: 98-70654

Harcourt Brace College Publishers may provide complimentary instructional aids and supplements or supplement packages to those adopters qualified under our adoption policy. Please contact your sales representative for more information. If as an adopter or potential user you receive supplements you do not need, please return them to your sales representative or send them to: Attn: Returns Department, Troy Warehouse, 465 South Lincoln Drive, Troy, MO 63379.

Address for orders:
Harcourt Brace & Company
6277 Sea Harbor Drive
Orlando, FL 32887-6777
1-800-782-4479

Address for editorial correspondence:
Harcourt Brace College Publishers
301 Commerce Street, Suite 3700
Fort Worth, TX 76102

Web site address:
http://www.hbcollege.com

Printed in the United States of America

8 9 0 1 2 3 4 5 6 7   066   9 8 7 6 5 4 3 2 1

ABOUT THE SERIES

The Harcourt Brace Casebook Series in Literature has its origins in our anthology *Literature: Reading, Reacting, Writing* (Third Edition, 1997), which in turn arose out of our many years of teaching college writing and literature courses. The primary purpose of each Casebook in the series is to offer students a convenient, self-contained reference tool that they can use to complete a research project for an introductory literature course.

In choosing subjects for the Casebooks, we draw on our own experience in the classroom, selecting works of poetry, fiction, and drama that students like to read, discuss, and write about and that teachers like to teach. Unlike other collections of literary criticism aimed at student audiences, The Harcourt Brace Casebook Series in Literature features short stories, groups of poems, or plays (rather than longer works, such as novels) because these are the genres most often taught in college-level Introduction to Literature courses. In selecting particular authors and titles, we focus on those most popular with students and those most accessible to them.

To facilitate student research—and to facilitate instructor supervision of that research—each Casebook contains all the resources students need to produce a documented research paper on a particular work of literature. Every Casebook in the series includes the following elements:

- A comprehensive **introduction** to the work, providing social, historical, and political background. This introduction helps students to understand the work and the author in the context of a particular time and place. In particular, the introduction enables students to appreciate customs, situations, and events that may have contributed to the author's choice of subject matter, emphasis, or style.

- A **headnote,** including birth and death dates of the author; details of the work's first publication and its subsequent publication history, if relevant; details about the author's life; a summary of the author's career; and a list of key published works, with dates of publication.

- The most widely accepted version of the **literary work,** along with the explanatory footnotes students will need to understand unfamiliar terms and concepts or references to people, places, or events.

- **Discussion questions** focusing on themes developed in the work. These questions, designed to stimulate critical thinking and discussion, can also serve as springboards for research projects.

- Several extended **research assignments** related to the literary work. Students may use these assignments exactly as they appear in the Casebook, or students or instructors may modify the assignments to suit their own needs or research interests.

- A diverse collection of traditional and non-traditional **secondary sources,** which may include scholarly articles, reviews, interviews, memoirs, newspaper articles, historical documents, and so on. This resource offers students access to sources they might not turn to on their own—for example, a popular song that inspired a short story, a story that was the original version of a play, a legal document that sheds light on a work's theme, or two different biographies of an author—thus encouraging students to look beyond the obvious or the familiar as they search for ideas. Students may use only these sources, or they may supplement them with sources listed in the Casebook's bibliography (see below).

- An annotated model **student research paper** drawing on several of the Casebook's secondary sources. This paper uses MLA parenthetical documentation and includes a Works Cited list conforming to MLA style.

- A comprehensive **bibliography** of print and electronic sources related to the work. This bibliography offers students an opportunity to move beyond the sources in the Casebook to other sources related to a particular research topic.

- A concise **guide to MLA documentation,** including information on what kinds of information require documentation (and what kinds do not); a full explanation of how to construct parenthetical references and how to place them in a paper; sample parenthetical reference formats for various kinds of sources used in papers about literature; a complete explanation of how to assemble a List of Works Cited, accompanied by sample works cited entries (including formats for documenting electronic sources); and guidelines for using explanatory notes (with examples).

By collecting all this essential information in one convenient place, each volume in The Harcourt Brace Casebook Series in Literature responds to the needs of both students and teachers. For students, the Casebooks offer convenience, referentiality, and portability that make the process of doing research easier. Thus, the Casebooks recognize what students already know: that Introduction to Literature is not their only class and that the literature research paper is not their only assignment. For instructors, the Casebooks offer a rare combination of flexibility and control in the classroom. For example, teachers may choose to assign one Casebook or more than one; thus, they have the option of having all students in a class write about the same work or having different groups of students, or individual students, write about different works. In addition, instructors may ask students to use only the secondary sources collected in the Casebook, thereby controlling students' use of (and acknowledgment of) sources more closely, or they may encourage students to seek both print and electronic sources beyond those included in the Casebook. By building convenience, structure, and flexibility into each volume, we have designed The Harcourt Brace Casebook Series in Literature to suit a wide variety of teaching styles and research interests. The Casebooks have made the research paper an easier project for us and a less stressful one for our students; we hope they will do the same for you.

Laurie G. Kirszner
Stephen R. Mandell
Series Editors

PREFACE

"The Yellow Wallpaper" was written by Charlotte Perkins Gilman at a time when many issues significant to women's lives in the United States were considered unimportant. Struggling against the Victorian model of woman as passive wife and mother, Gilman could not know that her story would both predict and reflect the gender role debates of the next hundred years. Despite modern society's broader acceptance of women's rights and capabilities, "The Yellow Wallpaper" remains a chilling reminder of the powerful force of social norms.

One wonders when reading "The Yellow Wallpaper": could this story take place today? Do Jane and John behave as husbands and wives do in society today? Do we view doctors as Jane and Jennie do? How sensitive are we to mental illness? The answers to these questions tell us much about our beliefs and values as individuals—and as a society.

The secondary sources included in this Casebook offer a variety of points of view about "The Yellow Wallpaper." Some offer historical perspectives, one is autobiographical, and others discuss literary devices or offer interpretations. All were selected to help you to understand this remarkable story and appreciate its characters and themes. The secondary sources are:

- Gilman, Charlotte Perkins. "Why I Wrote 'The Yellow Wallpaper'." Here Gilman discusses her reasons for writing the story and explains what she hoped to accomplish.

- Hedges, Elaine R. "Scudder's Comment on 'The Yellow Wallpaper.'" In an Afterword to The Feminist Press edition of "The Yellow Wallpaper," Hedges wrote of Gilman's efforts to publish the story, and describes its reception by at least one editor.

- From Gilbert, Sandra M. and Susan Gubar. *The Madwoman in the Attic: The Woman Writer and the Nineteenth Century Literary Imagination.* This selection explores the metaphors of confinement and escape that the authors see in the story.

- Lane, Ann J. "Silas Weir Mitchell," Chapter V of *To Herland and Beyond: The Life and Works of Charlotte Perkins Gilman*. This excerpt describes how women were viewed by the Victorian patriarchy and explains how those attitudes affected the medical treatment women received at the hands of male physicians.

- Hill, Mary A. "The Crown of Womanhood 1884–1887," Chapter 6 of *The Making of a Radical Feminist 1860–1896*. This biographical discussion sheds light on Gilman's concerns about marriage, motherhood, work and her health.

- Treichler, Paula A. "Escaping the Sentence: Diagnosis and Discourse in 'The Yellow Wallpaper'," in *Feminist Issues in Literary Scholarship*. This essay explores the concept of "sentence" in the story.

- Golden, Catherine. "'Overwriting' the Rest Cure: Charlotte Perkins Gilman's Literary Escape from S. Weir Mitchell's Fictionalization of Women." This essay, from *Critical Essays on Charlotte Perkins Gilman*, presents an interesting comparison of the doctor–patient relationship found in the fiction writing of Charlotte Perkins Gilman and of her doctor, Silas Weir Mitchell.

- Knight, Denise D. Chapter 12 of *The Diaries of Charlotte Perkins Gilman*. These entries from Gilman's diary offer her perspective on her life as she awaited the birth of her daughter, gave birth, and struggled with motherhood.

The Casebook also includes a student paper. This paper not only illustrates MLA documentation style, but also shows how the various sources in the Casebook can be used to write about "The Yellow Wallpaper." The student writer, Erin Justino, discusses a major issue of the short story—the role of women in society—as she examines the confinement and escape experienced by the main character, Jane. Notice that throughout the paper the critics' ideas supplement and support Erin's own ideas, but that her voice dominates the discussion.

ACKNOWLEDGMENTS

While writing is a solitary activity, the end product of that activity always involves collaborative efforts. And so I would like to thank all of the staff at Harcourt Brace: Michael Rosenberg, who suggested the idea of a Casebook series; Julie McBurney, the acquisitions editor; Andrea Wright, the project editor; Vicki Whistler, the art director; Linda McMillan, the production manager; and especially Katie Frushour, the developmental editor, for their expertise and patience during the creation of this Casebook. In addition, I would like to thank Laurie G. Kirszner and Stephen R. Mandell, senior editors of The Harcourt Brace Casebook Series. As well, I would like to thank my family and friends, who generously gave their support to my work on this project.

CONTENTS

Introduction

"The Yellow Wallpaper": A Story and a Life

"The Yellow Wallpaper" by Charlotte Perkins Gilman was written in 1892, when the position of women in U.S. society was very different from what it is today. Women could not vote. Education for women, especially higher education, was limited. Young women who worked in garment factories earned as little as 1¢ per hour, and these wages were legally owned by their fathers or husbands. A woman's legal and social status was based on her dependence upon the men around her, whether father, husband, factory owner, minister or doctor. This patriarchal social structure—a system that valued male-dominated lawmaking and male-determined social interaction—troubled Gilman, who worried about its effects on women. Readers will better understand Gilman's work, and especially "The Yellow Wallpaper," if they are aware of the economic, social and political forces that existed when the story was written.

TRUE WOMANHOOD

One of the most significant social forces of the 1890s was a cultural phenomenon then popularly known as True Womanhood. The Civil War, immigration, increased urbanization, and industrialization had created enormous changes in the lives of women in general, and especially in the lives of immigrant and lower-class working women. Nevertheless, most middle- and upper-class urban women, particularly in the Northeast—like the women Gilman wrote about in "The Yellow Wallpaper"—lived under the powerful influence of this social force.

True Womanhood established standards of behavior for a "lady." Women who wanted to be accepted, married, and valued by their society needed to adhere to the required behavior closely. Those women who chose not to follow True Womanhood, or to leave it, were often rejected by their

2

families and communities. A woman thus rejected was typically without resources or education and likely faced a dismal future.

According to the cult of True Womanhood, a "lady" acted out of piety derived from her religious beliefs, remained pure as a young woman and faithful when married, embodied the spirit of submissiveness, and committed her entire being to her domestic life, namely her husband and children.

Membership in a religious group and attendance at church were considered important for a lady or "true woman"; it was at church that she would learn the qualities of purity and submissiveness. Although most religious denominations welcomed both men and women, women were especially valued as the keepers and teachers of the faith in the home. Thus a woman who observed the beliefs of her religion was seen as more likely to be pure of intent and action than one who did not. Although a young man might try to lead her from the path of virtue and honesty or a husband might act in some petty way, a true woman knew how to resist such behavior and, if necessary, to forgive the sinful act and reestablish a pious and proper relationship.

Equally important, a true woman acted in a submissive manner within the family and society. When unmarried, she followed her father's rules and advice and went on to do the same with her husband—agreeably, not grudgingly. Her husband made all decisions for the family and felt no need to consult her, assuming both her agreement and her agreeability.

Lastly, the true woman dedicated herself selflessly to her family. She had no goals for herself that would detract from her role as wife, mother, and housekeeper. A woman whose children displayed good manners, whose home shone with cleanliness, whose hearth radiated the aroma of warm bread, whose husband smiled and prospered, was considered the highest form of being. Not only was such a true woman important to her family, but by extension she was responsible for the well-being of her community and society.

The enforcement of the values of true womanhood came from two sources. One line of influence came from European norms and the Victorian ideals popular in England in the 1890s. Many families in the eastern United States came from Europe or England, and they brought with them a religious heritage and their own standards of civilized human interaction. Queen Victoria of England was deeply admired, and with her pious bearing, was seen as a proper role model for the aspiring "lady."

Economic circumstances in the years immediately prior to the 1890s also helped dictate a more domestic role for women. When the Civil War ended, soldiers returned home to resume their jobs. Women who had been running offices, farms, and factories in their absence were told to return home in order to reestablish the proper social order and to take care of the children. Although most women were happy to accommodate, some had come to appreciate their economic independence.

Even if the requirements of True Womanhood seemed unacceptable to some middle- and upper-class women, most found the alternatives—social rejection and alienation—too high a price to pay for violating its precepts. A few, mainly abolitionists and suffragists (including Charlotte Perkins Gilman), did question this definition of womanhood and rebelled. Gilman left her husband and child and faced scathing criticism in the press, but she went on to create an independent life for herself.

WOMEN AND DIVORCE

One of the consequences women faced if they decided to rebel against the limiting definitions of womanhood and marriage was divorce. Although divorce was legal in the United States, the realities of divorce were harsh. A woman faced the possibility of losing some or all of her property in a divorce and, potentially even more devastating, she faced the loss of her children. Although equal division of property laws were enacted by several states after the Civil War, a woman was still dependent on a male judge's interpretation of those laws. A woman threatened by the loss of her assets by a judge friendly to her husband had little ability to appeal such an injustice.

Moreover, because a divorced woman was considered by the law to be both morally and economically deficient, custody of children was typically granted to the father. Even if a woman did win custody of her children, without support from a job or her family she would struggle to house and feed them. It comes as no surprise, then, that most middle- and upper-class women chose to adapt to the ideal of "true womanhood."

SILAS WEIR MITCHELL

The range of illnesses, especially of the nerves, suffered by large numbers of middle- and upper-class women during the 1890s leads us to suspect that conformity had its costs. Those women not able to adapt to the ideals of piety, purity, submissiveness, and domesticity suffered from exhaustion, depression, and hysteria, although neither the causes of nor the cures for these conditions were understood. Freud's theories of the unconscious and its power were only just being developed and had not reached the medical establishment. Still, most doctors (predominantly male) acknowledged the real effects of depression and hysteria and many, including one of the most well-known neurologists of the day, Silas Weir Mitchell, recognized the connection between mind and body.

Silas Weir Mitchell, in his mid-forties during the 1890s, had an international reputation as a neurologist and was highly regarded in the United States. His medical practice had made him rich, and women traveled from around the world to be treated by him. In addition to practicing medicine, he wrote medical books, novels, short stories, and poetry. Many reviewers considered him a versatile genius.

Raised by parents he loved deeply, Mitchell quarreled with his father over his choice of profession, and this caused the son great distress. Nevertheless the younger Mitchell pursued a medical career, and during the Civil War he worked in a hospital treating wounded soldiers. Here he began to learn about what he called "nerve wounds" and "nerve diseases." Mitchell himself suffered a nervous breakdown after the war when both his father and his new wife died within a short period, but after a second marriage, he established a medical practice in Philadelphia and began treating depressed women.

Although many doctors admitted they could not explain what caused nervous disorders, others theorized that they were a kind of "overload" that could be treated with medicine, leeches, and "rest cures." For his women patients, Silas Weir Mitchell prescribed bed rest, abstinence from physical and intellectual exertion, and no visits or interaction with family or friends. Many women, given a reprieve from the repressive emotional requirements of unending familial and social duties, did indeed recover and return to their homes to resume their lives. Some returned regularly for the rest cure.

Two of Mitchell's more well-known patients—social activist Jane Addams and writer Charlotte Perkins Gilman—did not recover, however, and in fact got worse while undergoing treatment. Gilman went to Mitchell after suffering depression for three years following the birth of her daughter. Not only did Gilman find caring for an infant overwhelming, but she also had personal goals that no one seemed to recognize or acknowledge. The goal of Mitchell's rest cure, and of all nervous disorder treatments was to return the woman to her role as wife and mother. If Gilman had recovered, she would have had to return to a position she found increasingly unbearable. And so Gilman rejected Silas Weir Mitchell's treatment, returned home, and then left to visit friends in California. In California her depression lifted, and she began the process of creating an independent life.

THE PUBLICATION AND RECEPTION OF "THE YELLOW WALLPAPER"

Out of this very personal experience came Gilman's story "The Yellow Wallpaper." The story chronicles a similar "rest cure" that takes place over a summer in a rundown country house. The rest cure is administered by the woman's husband, a doctor. Much like Gilman, the woman does not respond well to the cure, retreating instead into madness. Gilman later explained that she wrote the story and sent a copy of it to Mitchell to prevent anyone else from having to undergo a similar painful experience.

Some members of the medical profession praised the story as an accurate description of a mind slipping into madness. Mitchell himself admitted later in his career that Gilman's story forced him to re-examine his approach to female nervous disorder and to consider other treatment options. However, some of the first publishers to whom the story was submitted considered it too depressing for publication—perhaps because of its depiction of a husband's faulty interpretation of his wife's needs, and the terrible consequences of that interpretation.

Some early publishers of the story placed it within a then-popular genre called Gothic fiction, which included ghost stories and other tales of the supernatural. Gothic fiction writers, such as Ann Radcliffe in eighteenth-century England and Edith Wharton in the nineteenth-century United States, created stories characterized by gloomy settings and unexplained events, in which the protagonists (often women) struggled to escape from frightful forces. These stories, with their helpless, trapped heroines, mirrored women's lives. Thus, such writing often served to mask more subversive intents as these writers challenged and criticized the male-dominated society and its effects on women. The ghosts, curses, and supernatural events seen (or imagined) by the protagonists of these stories often served as symbols for women's desperate attempts to negotiate a world where gender inequities weighed heavily in so many areas of women's lives.

Some initial literary criticism of "The Yellow Wallpaper," then, saw it as a ghost story. Other critics simplistically looked at the setting of the story or at the wallpaper itself as the source of the wife's madness. Still other critics attributed Jane's madness to some disease of the nerves, seemingly beyond human control. None of these early interpretations, however, appreciated the importance of the husband-wife relationship or the interrelatedness of environment, post-partum depression, and the marriage/power relationship. With the development of feminist literary criticism in the 1970s, "The Yellow Wallpaper" would be rediscovered, reinterpreted, and revalued.

REDISCOVERY OF "THE YELLOW WALLPAPER"

The twentieth century saw vast changes in the position and status of women in the United States. First, second, and third generations of college-educated women joined the professions; women won the right to vote in 1920; and women joined the workforce in increasing numbers, gaining economic independence. During the 1970s a wave of feminism swept the country, giving names to and analyzing maladies and problems previously unnamed and ignored. Women social activists, thinkers, and writers spoke and marched and wrote about gender inequities from unequal pay to discriminatory health care to sexual harassment to domestic and social violence against women.

It was during this period that Gilman's "The Yellow Wallpaper" was reappraised as a powerful example of feminist writing in which the sexual politics of marriage and male–female power relations were exposed. Gilman could not have guessed that her literary masterpiece would both predict and reflect the gender debates of a century of US history.

WORKS CONSULTED

Chafe, William. *Women and Equality: Changing Patterns in American Culture.* New York: Oxford UP, 1977.

Davidson, Cathy N. and Linda Wagner-Martin, eds. *The Oxford Companion to Women's Writing in the United States.* New York: Oxford UP, 1995.

Degler, Carl N. *Out of Our Past: The Forces That Shaped Modern America.* New York: Harper, 1984.

Ehrenreich, Barbara and Deidre English. *Complaints and Disorders: The Sexual Politics of Illness.* New York: Glass Mountain Pamphlet No. 2, *Feminist,* 1973.

Evans, Sara. *Personal Politics: The Roots of Women's Liberation in the Civil Rights Movement and the New Left.* New York: Knopf, 1979.

Flexner, Eleanor. *A Century of Struggle.* Cambridge: Harvard UP, 1975.

Gilman, Charlotte Perkins. *Women and Economics.* New York: Harper, 1966.

Heineman, Sue. *Timelines of American Women's History.* New York: Berkeley Publishing Group, 1996.

Hymowitz, Carol and Michaele Weissman. *A History of Women in America.* New York: Bantam, 1978.

Ryan, Mary P. *Womanhood in America: From Colonial Times to Present.* 2nd ed. New York: Viewpoint, 1979.

Zinn, Howard. *A People's History of the United States.* New York: Harper, 1990.

Literature

About the Author

CHARLOTTE PERKINS GILMAN (1860–1935), writer, social philosopher, and lecturer, spent most of her life working for the social and economic equality of women. She sought to bridge the gap between the private world of home and the public world of work so that women might develop into whole, fully realized selves. Although she achieved considerable professional acclaim and success in her work, Gilman endured tension and struggle in her personal life.

Born in Hartford, Connecticut, into a family of social activists and thinkers that included Harriet Beecher Stowe, Gilman wrote in her autobiography, *The Living of Charlotte Perkins Gilman* (1935), "I was bent on doing my best, and eager for self-improvement." But the general circumstances of Gilman's life created obstacles to her desire. Her mother, Mary A. Perkins, decided to teach young Charlotte about the harshness of life at an early age and refused to hold or kiss her daughter. Gilman's father, unable to support his family in a consistent manner, finally left them when Charlotte was thirteen. Gilman viewed her childhood as unhappy and believed that it led to some of the anxiety she experienced as an adult. Those same early life experiences, however, also taught her an independence of mind that would lead to some of her most satisfying professional successes.

Charlotte Perkins received basic schooling from both her mother and her father. Later, she attended the Rhode Island School of Design, where she became interested in painting and drawing. At age twenty-two she met and was courted by a young artist, Charles Walter Stetson, and began struggling with concerns about being able to maintain an autonomous, working self within a traditional marriage. Despite her concerns, she married Stetson in 1884, and their daughter Katharine was born a year later.

After Katharine's birth, Gilman suffered depression that went unrelieved for three years. She finally agreed to the "rest cure" prescribed by the renowned Philadelphia neurologist Dr. Silas Weir Mitchell. Forced to rest, sleep, do nothing, and see no one, Gilman's depression grew worse and she eventually returned to her family. Told to resume a totally homebound, domestic lifestyle, Gilman decided that remaining in her marriage would drive her insane, and she left. Visiting friends in California, she recovered her sanity and her health, but her divorce and her decision to send Katharine to live with Walter and his new wife generated tremendous negative publicity for Gilman.

Out of this experience came "The Yellow Wallpaper." Written in 1892 and marking the beginning of Gilman's life as a writer, philosopher, and lecturer, the story was read originally as a horror tale in the tradition of Nathaniel Hawthorne and Edgar Allan Poe, not as an indictment of male-dominated society. Six years later, Gilman published her best-known work, *Women and Economics*. Eventually translated into seven languages, *Women and Economics* argued that women's economic dependence on men not only doomed them to live stifled lives but also retarded the development of the human species. *Women and Economics* established Charlotte Perkins Gilman as the leading feminist theorist of the early twentieth century.

In 1900, Charlotte Perkins Stetson married her cousin George Gilman, who respected her scholarly work and was able to help create the household arrangements needed by his now highly in demand working wife. In *Concerning Children* (1900), *The Home* (1904), and *Human Work* (1904), Gilman advocated such revolutionary ideas as day care centers, the professionalization of housework, and centralized food preparation. In *Man-Made World* (1911) and *His Religion and Hers* (1923), she affirmed women as the superior form of the human species because of their commitment to life, as opposed to men's preoccupation with war. For seven years ending in 1916, Gilman wrote, edited, and published a monthly magazine called *Forerunner*. In it she serialized *Herland* (1915), a fantasy novel about a feminist utopia inhabited solely by women.

As her reputation grew, Gilman traveled and lectured throughout the United States and Europe on behalf of women's social and economic equality and their right to vote. She realized that winning the right to vote in 1920, although important, was insignificant as long as women did not have economic equality. She thus encouraged women of all ages to seek education and professional training, to work in any field they chose, and to maintain control of their money.

As the interests of women and society changed in the 1920s and 1930s, Gilman began to lose her audience. She failed to comprehend the growing importance of women's increased social independence and the significance of the Depression, and as a result, her writing no longer reflected the realities of the lives of growing numbers of middle-class women who divorced, lived independent lives, or simply struggled to earn a living.

When her husband died unexpectedly in 1934, Gilman returned to California to live near her daughter. In 1935 Gilman took her own life, with chloroform. In a note left for her daughter, Gilman stated that she chose this course not because of the breast cancer she suffered but because she felt her capacity for service was ended.

In the years following her death, Gilman's work went unread and eventually went out of print. In the 1970s, however, feminist writers and theorists rediscovered and reappraised Gilman's work. "The Yellow Wallpaper" in particular has generated much interest as modern readers appreciate both its literary merit and its profound social commentary.

The Yellow Wallpaper
(1899)

1 It is very seldom that mere ordinary people like John and myself secure ancestral halls for the summer.

A colonial mansion, a hereditary estate, I would say a haunted house, and reach the height of romantic felicity—but that would be asking too much of fate!

Still I will proudly declare that there is something queer about it.

Else, why should it be let so cheaply? And why have stood so long untenanted?

5 John laughs at me, of course, but one expects that in marriage.

John is practical in the extreme. He has no patience with faith, an intense horror of superstition, and he scoffs openly at any talk of things not to be felt and seen and put down in figures.

John is a physician, and *perhaps*—(I would not say it to a living soul, of course, but this is dead paper and a great relief to my mind—) *perhaps* that is one reason I do not get well faster.

You see he does not believe I am sick!

And what can one do?

10 If a physician of high standing, and one's own husband, assures friends and relatives that there is really nothing the matter with one but temporary nervous depression—a slight hysterical tendency—what is one to do?

My brother is also a physician, and also of high standing, and he says the same thing.

So I take phosphates or phosphites[1]—whichever it is, and tonics, and journeys, and air, and exercise, and am absolutely forbidden to "work" until I am well again.

---

[1] Both terms refer to salts of phosphorous acid. The narrator, however, means "phosphate," a carbonated beverage of water, flavoring, and a small amount of phosphoric acid.

Personally, I disagree with their ideas.

Personally, I believe that congenial work, with excitement and change, would do me good.

15 But what is one to do?

I did write for a while in spite of them; but it *does* exhaust me a good deal—having to be so sly about it, or else meet with heavy opposition.

I sometimes fancy that in my condition if I had less opposition and more society and stimulus—but John says the very worst thing I can do is to think about my condition, and I confess it always makes me feel bad.

So I will let it alone and talk about the house.

The most beautiful place! It is quite alone, standing well back from the road, quite three miles from the village. It makes me think of English places that you read about, for there are hedges and walls and gates that lock, and lots of separate little houses for the gardeners and people.

20 There is a *delicious* garden! I never saw such a garden—large and shady, full of box-bordered paths, and lined with long grape-covered arbors with seats under them.

There were greenhouses, too, but they are all broken now.

There was some legal trouble, I believe, something about the heirs and co-heirs; anyhow, the place has been empty for years.

That spoils my ghostliness, I am afraid, but I don't care—there is something strange about the house—I can feel it.

I even said so to John one moonlight evening, but he said what I felt was a *draught,* and shut the window.

25 I get unreasonably angry with John sometimes. I'm sure I never used to be so sensitive. I think it is due to this nervous condition.

But John says if I feel so, I shall neglect proper self-control; so I take pains to control myself—before him, at least, and that makes me very tired.

I don't like our room a bit. I wanted one downstairs that opened on the piazza and had roses all over the window, and such pretty old-fashioned chintz hangings! But John would not hear of it.

He said there was only one window and not room for two beds, and no near room for him if he took another.

He is very careful and loving, and hardly lets me stir without special direction.

30 I have a schedule prescription for each hour in the day; he takes all care from me, and so I feel basely ungrateful not to value it more.

He said we came here solely on my account, that I was to have perfect rest and all the air I could get. "Your exercise depends on your strength, my dear," said he, "and your food somewhat on your appetite; but air you can absorb all the time." So we took the nursery at the top of the house.

It is a big, airy room, the whole floor nearly, with windows that look all ways, and air and sunshine galore. It was nursery first and then playroom and gymnasium, I should judge; for the windows are barred for little children, and there are rings and things in the walls.

The paint and paper look as if a boys' school had used it. It is stripped off—the paper—in great patches all around the head of my bed, about as far as I can reach, and in a great place on the other side of the room low down. I never saw a worse paper in my life.

One of those sprawling flamboyant patterns committing every artistic sin.

35   It is dull enough to confuse the eye in following, pronounced enough to constantly irritate and provoke study, and when you follow the lame uncertain curves for a little distance they suddenly commit suicide—plunge off at outrageous angles, destroy themselves in unheard of contradictions.

The color is repellent, almost revolting; a smouldering unclean yellow, strangely faded by the slow-turning sunlight.

It is a dull yet lurid orange in some places, a sickly sulphur tint in others.

No wonder the children hated it! I should hate it myself if I had to live in this room long.

There comes John, and I must put this away,—he hates to have me write a word.

40   We have been here two weeks, and I haven't felt like writing before, since that first day.

I am sitting by the window now, up in this atrocious nursery, and there is nothing to hinder my writing as much as I please, save lack of strength.

John is away all day, and even some nights when his cases are serious.

I am glad my case is not serious!

But these nervous troubles are dreadfully depressing.

45   John does not know how much I really suffer. He knows there is no *reason* to suffer, and that satisfies him.

Of course it is only nervousness. It does weigh on me so not to do my duty in any way!

I meant to be such a help to John, such a real rest and comfort, and here I am a comparative burden already!

Nobody would believe what an effort it is to do what little I am able,— to dress and entertain, and order things.

It is fortunate Mary is so good with the baby. Such a dear baby!

50   And yet I *cannot* be with him, it makes me so nervous.

I suppose John never was nervous in his life. He laughs at me so about this wallpaper!

At first he meant to repaper the room, but afterwards he said that I was letting it get the better of me, and that nothing was worse for a nervous patient than to give way to such fancies.

He said that after the wallpaper was changed it would be the heavy bedstead, and then the barred windows, and then that gate at the head of the stairs, and so on.

"You know the place is doing you good," he said, "and really, dear, I don't care to renovate the house just for a three months' rental."

"Then do let us go downstairs," I said, "there are such pretty rooms there."

Then he took me in his arms and called me a blessed little goose, and said he would go down cellar, if I wished, and have it whitewashed into the bargain.

But he is right enough about the beds and windows and things.

It is an airy and comfortable room as any one need wish, and, of course, I would not be so silly as to make him uncomfortable just for a whim.

I'm really getting quite fond of the big room, all but that horrid paper.

Out of one window I can see the garden, those mysterious deep-shaded arbors, the riotous old-fashioned flowers, and bushes and gnarly trees.

Out of another I get a lovely view of the bay and a little private wharf belonging to the estate. There is a beautiful shaded lane that runs down there from the house. I always fancy I see people walking in these numerous paths and arbors, but John has cautioned me not to give way to fancy in the least. He says that with my imaginative power and habit of story-making, a nervous weakness like mine is sure to lead to all manner of excited fancies, and that I ought to use my will and good sense to check the tendency. So I try.

I think sometimes that if I were only well enough to write a little it would relieve the press of ideas and rest me.

But I find I get pretty tired when I try.

It is so discouraging not to have any advice and companionship about my work. When I get really well, John says we will ask Cousin Henry and Julia down for a long visit; but he says he would as soon put fireworks in my pillow-case as to let me have those stimulating people about now.

I wish I could get well faster.

But I must not think about that. This paper looks to me as if it *knew* what a vicious influence it had!

There is a recurrent spot where the pattern lolls like a broken neck and two bulbous eyes stare at you upside down.

I get positively angry with the impertinence of it and the everlastingness. Up and down and sideways they crawl, and those absurd, unblinking eyes are everywhere. There is one place where two breadths didn't match, and the eyes go all up and down the line, one a little higher than the other.

I never saw so much expression in an inanimate thing before, and we all know how much expression they have! I used to lie awake as a child and get more entertainment and terror out of blank walls and plain furniture than most children could find in a toy-store.

70   I remember what a kindly wink the knobs of our big, old bureau used to have, and there was one chair that always seemed like a strong friend.

I used to feel that if any of the other things looked too fierce I could always hop into that chair and be safe.

The furniture in this room is no worse than inharmonious, however, for we had to bring it all from downstairs. I suppose when this was used as a playroom they had to take the nursery things out, and no wonder! I never saw such ravages as the children have made here.

The wallpaper, as I said before, is torn off in spots, and it sticketh closer than a brother—they must have had perseverance as well as hatred.

Then the floor is scratched and gouged and splintered, the plaster itself is dug out here and there, and this great heavy bed which is all we found in the room, looks as if it had been through the wars.

75   But I don't mind it a bit—only the paper.

There comes John's sister. Such a dear girl as she is, and so careful of me! I must not let her find me writing.

She is a perfect and enthusiastic housekeeper, and hopes for no better profession. I verily believe she thinks it is the writing which made me sick!

But I can write when she is out, and see her a long way off from these windows.

There is one that commands the road, a lovely shaded winding road, and one that just looks off over the country. A lovely country, too, full of great elms and velvet meadows.

80   This wallpaper has a kind of sub-pattern in a different shade, a particularly irritating one, for you can only see it in certain lights, and not clearly then.

But in the places where it isn't faded and where the sun is just so—I can see a strange, provoking, formless sort of figure, that seems to skulk about behind that silly and conspicuous front design.

There's sister on the stairs!

Well, the Fourth of July is over! The people are all gone and I am tired out. John thought it might do me good to see a little company, so we just had mother and Nellie and the children down for a week.

Of course I didn't do a thing. Jennie sees to everything now.

But it tired me all the same.

John says if I don't pick up faster he shall send me to Weir Mitchell[2] in the fall.

But I don't want to go there at all. I had a friend who was in his hands once, and she says he is just like John and my brother, only more so!

Besides, it is such an undertaking to go so far.

I don't feel as if it was worth while to turn my hand over for anything, and I'm getting dreadfully fretful and querulous.

I cry at nothing, and cry most of the time.

Of course I don't when John is here, or anybody else, but when I am alone.

And I am alone a good deal just now. John is kept in town very often by serious cases, and Jennie is good and lets me alone when I want her to.

So I walk a little in the garden or down that lovely lane, sit on the porch under the roses, and lie down up here a good deal.

I'm getting really fond of the room in spite of the wallpaper. Perhaps *because* of the wallpaper.

It dwells in my mind so!

I lie here on this great immovable bed—it is nailed down, I believe—and follow that pattern about by the hour. It is as good as gymnastics, I assure you. I start, we'll say, at the bottom, down in the corner over there where it has not been touched, and I determine for the thousandth time that I *will* follow that pointless pattern to some sort of a conclusion.

I know a little of the principle of design, and I know this thing was not arranged on any laws of radiation, or alternation, or repetition, or symmetry, or anything else that I ever heard of.

It is repeated, of course, by the breadths, but not otherwise.

Looked at in one way each breadth stands alone, the bloated curves and flourishes—a kind of "debased Romanesque" with *delirium tremens*[3] go waddling up and down in isolated columns of fatuity.

But, on the other hand, they connect diagonally, and the sprawling outlines run off in great slanting waves of optic horror, like a lot of wallowing seaweeds in full chase.

---

2 Silas Weir Mitchell (1829–1914)—a Philadelphia neurologist-psychologist who introduced the "rest cure" for nervous diseases.

3 Mental confusion caused by alcohol poisoning and characterized by physical tremors and hallucinations.

The whole thing goes horizontally, too, at least it seems so, and I exhaust myself in trying to distinguish the order of its going in that direction.

They have used a horizontal breadth for a frieze, and that adds wonderfully to the confusion.

There is one end of the room where it is almost intact, and there, when the crosslights fade and the low sun shines directly upon it, I can almost fancy radiation after all,—the interminable grotesques seems to form around a common center and rush off in headlong plunges of equal distraction.

It makes me tired to follow it. I will take a nap I guess.

105   I don't know why I should write this.

I don't want to.

I don't feel able.

And I know John would think it absurd. But I *must* say what I feel and think in some way—it is such a relief!

But the effort is getting to be greater than the relief.

110   Half the time now I am awfully lazy, and lie down ever so much.

John says I mustn't lose my strength, and has me take cod liver oil and lots of tonics and things, to say nothing of ale and wine and rare meat.

Dear John! He loves me very dearly, and hates to have me sick. I tried to have a real earnest reasonable talk with him the other day, and tell him how I wish he would let me go and make a visit to Cousin Henry and Julia.

But he said I wasn't able to go, nor able to stand it after I got there; and I did not make out a very good case for myself, for I was crying before I had finished.

It is getting to be a great effort for me to think straight. Just this nervous weakness I suppose.

115   And dear John gathered me up in his arms, and just carried me upstairs and laid me on the bed, and sat by me and read to me till it tired my head.

He said I was his darling and his comfort and all he had, and that I must take care of myself for his sake, and keep well.

He says no one but myself can help me out of it, that I must use my will and self-control and not let any silly fancies run away with me.

There's one comfort, the baby is well and happy, and does not have to occupy this nursery with the horrid wallpaper.

If we had not used it, that blessed child would have! What a fortunate escape! Why, I wouldn't have a child of mine, an impressionable little thing, live in such a room for worlds.

120   I never thought of it before, but it is lucky that John kept me here after all, I can stand it so much easier than a baby, you see.

Of course I never mention it to them any more—I am too wise,—but I keep watch of it all the same.

There are things in that paper that nobody knows but me, or ever will.

Behind that outside pattern the dim shapes get clearer every day.

It is always the same shape, only very numerous.

125 And it is like a woman stooping down and creeping about behind that pattern. I don't like it a bit. I wonder—I begin to think—I wish John would take me away from here!

It is so hard to talk with John about my case, because he is so wise, and because he loves me so.

But I tried it last night.

It was moonlight. The moon shines in all around just as the sun does.

I hate to see it sometimes, it creeps so slowly, and always comes in by one window or another.

130 John was asleep and I hated to waken him, so I kept still and watched the moonlight on that undulating wallpaper till I felt creepy.

The faint figure behind seemed to shake the pattern, just as if she wanted to get out.

I got up softly and went to feel and see if the paper *did* move, and when I came back John was awake.

"What is it, little girl?" he said. "Don't go walking about like that— you'll get cold."

I thought it was a good time to talk, so I told him that I really was not gaining here, and that I wished he would take me away.

135 "Why, darling!" said he, "our lease will be up in three weeks, and I can't see how to leave before.

"The repairs are not done at home, and I cannot possibly leave town just now. Of course if you were in any danger, I could and would, but you really are better, dear, whether you can see it or not. I am a doctor, dear, and I know. You are gaining flesh and color, your appetite is better, I feel really much easier about you."

"I don't weigh a bit more," said I, "nor as much; and my appetite may be better in the evening when you are here, but it is worse in the morning when you are away!"

"Bless her little heart!" said he with a big hug, "she shall be as sick as she pleases! But now let's improve the shining hours by going to sleep, and talk about it in the morning!"

"And you won't go away?" I asked gloomily.

140 "Why, how can I, dear? It is only three weeks more and then we will

take a nice little trip of a few days while Jennie is getting the house ready. Really dear you are better!"

"Better in body perhaps—" I began, and stopped short, for he sat up straight and looked at me with such a stern, reproachful look that I could not say another word.

"My darling," said he, "I beg of you, for my sake and for our child's sake, as well as for your own, that you will never for one instant let that idea enter your mind! There is nothing so dangerous, so fascinating, to a temperament like yours. It is a false and foolish fancy. Can you not trust me as a physician when I tell you so?"

So of course I said no more on that score, and we went to sleep before long. He thought I was asleep first, but I wasn't, and lay there for hours trying to decide whether that front pattern and the back pattern really did move together or separately.

On a pattern like this, by daylight, there is a lack of sequence, a defiance of law, that is a constant irritant to a normal mind.

145   The color is hideous enough, and unreliable enough, and infuriating enough, but the pattern is torturing.

You think you have mastered it, but just as you get well underway in following, it turns back-somersault and there you are. It slaps you in the face, knocks you down, and tramples upon you. It is like a bad dream.

The outside pattern is a florid arabesque, reminding one of a fungus. If you can imagine a toadstool in joints, an interminable string of toadstools, budding and sprouting in endless convolutions—why, that is something like it.

That is, sometimes!

There is one marked peculiarity about this paper, a thing nobody seems to notice but myself, and that is that it changes as the light changes.

150   When the sun shoots in through the east window—I always watch for that first long, straight ray—it changes so quickly that I never can quite believe it.

That is why I watch it always.

By moonlight—the moon shines in all night when there is a moon— I wouldn't know it was the same paper.

At night in any kind of light, in twilight, candlelight, lamplight, and worst of all by moonlight, it becomes bars! The outside pattern I mean, and the woman behind it is as plain as can be.

I didn't realize for a long time what the thing was that showed behind, that dim sub-pattern, but now I am quite sure it is a woman.

155   By daylight she is subdued, quiet. I fancy it is the pattern that keeps her so still. It is so puzzling. It keeps me quiet by the hour.

I lie down ever so much now. John says it is good for me, and to sleep all I can.

Indeed he started the habit by making me lie down for an hour after each meal.

It is a very bad habit I am convinced, for you see I don't sleep.

And that cultivates deceit, for I don't tell them I'm awake—O no!

160   The fact is I am getting a little afraid of John.

He seems very queer sometimes, and even Jennie has an inexplicable look.

It strikes me occasionally, just as a scientific hypothesis,—that perhaps it is the paper!

I have watched John when he did not know I was looking, and come into the room suddenly on the most innocent excuses, and I've caught him several times *looking at the paper!* And Jennie too. I caught Jennie with her hand on it once.

She didn't know I was in the room, and when I asked her in a quiet, a very quiet voice, with the most restrained manner possible, what she was doing with the paper—she turned around as if she had been caught stealing, and looked quite angry—asked me why I should frighten her so!

165   Then she said that the paper stained everything it touched, that she had found yellow smooches on all my clothes and John's, and she wished we would be more careful!

Did not that sound innocent? But I know she was studying that pattern, and I am determined that nobody shall find it out but myself!

Life is very much more exciting now than it used to be. You see I have something more to expect, to look forward to, to watch. I really do eat better, and am more quiet than I was.

John is so pleased to see me improve! He laughed a little the other day, and said I seemed to be flourishing in spite of my wallpaper.

I turned it off with a laugh. I had no intention of telling him it was *because* of the wallpaper—he would make fun of me. He might even want to take me away.

170   I don't want to leave now until I have found it out. There is a week more, and I think that will be enough.

I'm feeling ever so much better! I don't sleep much at night, for it is so interesting to watch developments; but I sleep a good deal in the daytime.

In the daytime it is tiresome and perplexing.

There are always new shoots on the fungus, and new shades of yellow all over it. I cannot keep count of them, though I have tried conscientiously.

It is the strangest yellow, that wallpaper! It makes me think of all the yellow things I ever saw—not beautiful ones like buttercups, but old foul, bad yellow things.

175   But there is something else about that paper—the smell! I noticed it the moment we came into the room, but with so much air and sun it was not bad. Now we have had a week of fog and rain, and whether the windows are open or not, the smell is here.

It creeps all over the house.

I find it hovering in the dining-room, skulking in the parlor, hiding in the hall, lying in wait for me on the stairs.

It gets into my hair.

Even when I go to ride, if I turn my head suddenly and surprise it—there is that smell!

180   Such a peculiar odor, too! I have spent hours in trying to analyze it, to find what it smelled like.

It is not bad—at first, and very gentle, but quite the subtlest, most enduring odor I ever met.

In this damp weather it is awful, I wake up in the night and find it hanging over me.

It used to disturb me at first. I thought seriously of burning the house—to reach the smell.

But now I am used to it. The only thing I can think of that it is like is the *color* of the paper! A yellow smell.

185   There is a very funny mark on this wall, low down, near the mop-board. A streak that runs round the room. It goes behind every piece of furniture, except the bed, a long, straight, even *smooch*, as if it had been rubbed over and over.

I wonder how it was done and who did it, and what they did it for. Round and round and round—round and round and round!—it makes me dizzy!

I really have discovered something at last.

Through watching so much at night, when it changes so, I have finally found out.

The front pattern *does* move—and no wonder! The woman behind shakes it!

190   Sometimes I think there are a great many women behind, and sometimes only one, and she crawls around fast, and her crawling shakes it all over.

Then in the very bright spots she keeps still, and in the very shady spots she just takes hold of the bars and shakes them hard.

And she is all the time trying to climb through. But nobody could climb through that pattern—it strangles so; I think that is why it has so many heads.

They get through, and then the pattern strangles them off and turns them upside down, and makes their eyes white!

If those heads were covered or taken off it would not be half so bad.

195   I think that woman gets out in the daytime!

And I'll tell you why—privately—I've seen her!

I can see her out of every one of my windows!

It is the same woman, I know, for she is always creeping, and most women do not creep by daylight.

I see her in that long shaded lane, creeping up and down. I see her in those dark grape arbors, creeping all around the garden.

200   I see her on that long road under the trees, creeping along, and when a carriage comes she hides under the blackberry vines.

I don't blame her a bit. It must be very humiliating to be caught creeping by daylight!

I always lock the door when I creep by daylight. I can't do it at night, for I know John would suspect something at once.

And John is so queer now, that I don't want to irritate him. I wish he would take another room! Besides, I don't want anybody to get that woman out at night but myself.

I often wonder if I could see her out of all the windows at once.

205   But, turn as fast as I can, I can only see out of one at one time.

And though I always see her, she *may* be able to creep faster than I can turn!

I have watched her sometimes away off in the open country, creeping as fast as a cloud shadow in a high wind.

If only that top pattern could be gotten off from the under one! I mean to try it, little by little.

I have found out another funny thing, but I shan't tell it this time! It does not do to trust people too much.

210   There are only two more days to get this paper off, and I believe John is beginning to notice. I don't like the look in his eyes.

And I heard him ask Jennie a lot of professional questions about me. She had a very good report to give.

She said I slept a good deal in the daytime.

John knows I don't sleep very well at night, for all I'm so quiet!

He asked me all sorts of questions, too, and pretended to be very loving and kind.

215 As if I couldn't see through him!

Still, I don't wonder he acts so, sleeping under this paper for three months.

It only interests me, but I feel sure John and Jennie are secretly affected by it.

Hurrah! This is the last day, but it is enough. John to stay in town over night, and won't be out until this evening.

Jennie wanted to sleep with me—the sly thing! But I told her I should undoubtedly rest better for a night all alone.

220 That was clever, for really I wasn't alone a bit! As soon as it was moonlight and that poor thing began to crawl and shake the pattern, I got up and ran to help her.

I pulled and she shook, I shook and she pulled, and before morning we had peeled off yards of that paper.

A strip about as high as my head and half around the room.

And then when the sun came and that awful pattern began to laugh at me, I declared I would finish it to-day!

We go away to-morrow, and they are moving all my furniture down again to leave things as they were before.

225 Jennie looked at the wall in amazement, but I told her merrily that I did it out of pure spite at the vicious thing.

She laughed and said she wouldn't mind doing it herself, but I must not get tired.

How she betrayed herself that time!

But I am here, and no person touches this paper but me,—not *alive!*

She tried to get me out of the room—it was too patent! But I said it was so quiet and empty and clean now that I believed I would lie down again and sleep all I could; and not to wake me even for dinner—I would call when I woke.

230 So now she is gone, and the servants are gone, and the things are gone, and there is nothing left but that great bedstead nailed down, with the canvas mattress we found on it.

We shall sleep downstairs to-night, and take the boat home tomorrow.

I quite enjoy the room, now it is bare again.

How those children did tear about here!

This bedstead is fairly gnawed!

235 But I must get to work.

I have locked the door and thrown the key down into the front path.

I don't want to go out, and I don't want to have anybody come in, till John comes.

I want to astonish him.

I've got a rope up here that even Jennie did not find. If that woman does get out, and tries to get away, I can tie her!

240 But I forgot I could not reach far without anything to stand on!

This bed will *not* move!

I tried to lift and push it until I was lame, and then I got so angry I bit off a little piece at one corner—but it hurt my teeth.

Then I peeled off all the paper I could reach standing on the floor. It sticks horribly and the pattern just enjoys it! All those strangled heads and bulbous eyes and waddling fungus growths just shriek with derision!

I am getting angry enough to do something desperate. To jump out of the window would be admirable exercise, but the bars are too strong even to try.

245 Besides I wouldn't do it. Of course not. I know well enough that a step like that is improper and might be misconstrued.

I don't like to *look* out of the windows even—there are so many of those creeping women, and they creep so fast.

I wonder if they come out of the wall-paper as I did?

But I am securely fastened now by my well-hidden rope—you don't get *me* out in the road there!

I suppose I shall have to get back behind the pattern when it comes night, and that is hard!

250 It is so pleasant to be out in this great room and creep around as I please!

I don't want to go outside. I won't, even if Jennie asks me to.

For outside you have to creep on the ground, and everything is green instead of yellow.

But here I can creep smoothly on the floor, and my shoulder just fits in that long smooch around the wall, so I cannot lose my way.

Why there's John at the door!

255 It is no use, young man, you can't open it!

How he does call and pound!

Now he's crying for an axe.

It would be a shame to break down that beautiful door!

"John dear!" said I in the gentlest voice, "the key is down by the front steps, under a plantain leaf!"

260 That silenced him for a few moments.

Then he said—very quietly indeed. "Open the door, my darling!"

"I can't," said I. "The key is down by the front door under a plantain leaf!"

And then I said it again, several times, very gently and slowly, and said it so often that he had to go and see, and he got it of course, and came in. He stopped short by the door.

"What is the matter?" he cried. "For God's sake, what are you doing!"

I kept on creeping just the same, but I looked at him over my shoulder.

"I've got out at last," said I, "in spite of you and Jane. And I've pulled off most of the paper, so you can't put me back!"

Now why should that man have fainted? But he did, and right across my path by the wall, so that I had to creep over him every time!

Discussion Questions

1. The ending of this story leaves much unanswered. What do you think might happen in the hours or days after John recovers consciousness?

2. Explain how a woman today might respond differently to the advice given by a husband (or doctor) such as the one in this story.

3. The setting for this story includes a remodeled children's nursery with barred windows and a bed nailed to the floor. How might these affect an occupant?

4. What do these comments reveal about the relationship between the husband and wife?

   "John laughs at me, of course, but one expects that in marriage." (5)

   "You see he does not believe I am sick." (8)

   "Then he took me in his arms and called me a blessed little goose . . ." (56)

5. Describe the wallpaper in your own words. Why does it become so offensive to the narrator? Why do you believe or not believe what she says about it?

6. The narrator of this story becomes insane by the end of the story. Choose several sentences that describe her mental deterioration. Why does her physician–husband apparently not recognize or acknowledge these clues?

7. Could the events in this story happen today? To support your position, explain what has and has not changed since this story was written.

8. The narrator is the protagonist of this story, and her husband John is the antagonist. Are there other characters or forces pitted against the narrator?

9. Notice all the references in this story to the narrator's "tiredness" or fatigue. What do you think makes her so tired?

10. How might this story be different if John, the doctor–husband, told it?

Research Questions

1. View the Tony Romain film version of "The Yellow Wallpaper," and compare it with the story. How is the film similar to or different from the story? Why might the filmmaker have interpreted or photographed the story in the way he did?

2. Read Toni Morrison's *Beloved*, a more modern ghost story. Compare the appearance and purpose of Beloved to the woman behind the wallpaper. How does each ghost help the main character express what she has previously been unable to express?

3. In her explanation of why she wrote "The Yellow Wallpaper," Gilman rejoiced that her story prompted Dr. Silas Weir Mitchell to alter his treatment of neurasthenia, the illness Gilman suffered after the birth of her daughter. Investigate neurasthenia in books like Barbara Ehrenlich's *Complaints and Disorders: The Sexual Politics of Illness*. Discuss how this illness was understood then and how it has been reinterpreted today.

4. In their selection from *The Madwoman in the Attic*, Sandra M. Gilbert and Susan Gubar discuss women writers' "parallel confinements in texts, house, and maternal female bodies" and the sometimes contorted escapes from such a "numb world" these writers fashioned. Analyze the various types of confinement and escape experienced by Jane in "The Yellow Wallpaper" in light of Gilbert and Gubar's assertions.

5. Gilman achieved international fame with her non-fiction work entitled *Women and Economics*. In it she argued for women's economic independence. Investigate this concept in *Women and Economics,* and discuss how Gilman's proposed reforms would change women's roles in society today.

6. In Mary Hill's *Charlotte Perkins Gilman: The Making of a Radical Feminist* and Paula Treichler's *Escaping the Sentence*, both critics discuss women's challenges finding adequate means of self-expression, especially in regard to the use of language. Discuss how Jane's self-expression in speaking and writing is limited, distorted, or ignored in "The Yellow Wallpaper." How might the story be different if Jane could speak and be heard in a more complete manner? Use Hill's and Treichler's articles to support your ideas.

Secondary Sources

Why I Wrote "The Yellow Wallpaper"
(1913)

Many and many a reader has asked that. When the story first came out, in the *New England Magazine* about 1891, a Boston physician made protest in *The Transcript*. Such a story ought not to be written, he said; it was enough to drive anyone mad to read it.

Another physician, in Kansas I think, wrote to say that it was the best description of incipient insanity he had ever seen, and—begging my pardon—had I been there?

Now the story of the story is this:

For many years I suffered from a severe and continuous nervous break-down tending to melancholia—and beyond. During about the third year of this trouble I went, in devout faith and some faint stir of hope, to a noted specialist in nervous diseases, the best known in the country. This wise man put me to bed and applied the rest cure, to which a still-good physique responded so promptly that he concluded there was nothing much the matter with me, and sent me home with solemn advice to "live as domestic a life as far as possible," to "have but two hours' intellectual life a day," and "never to touch pen, brush, or pencil again" as long as I lived. This was in 1887.

I went home and obeyed those directions for some three months, and came so near the borderline of utter mental ruin that I could see over.

Then, using the remnants of intelligence that remained, and helped by a wise friend, I cast the noted specialist's advice to the winds and went to work again—work, the normal life of every human being; work, in which is joy and growth and service, without which one is a pauper and a parasite—ultimately recovering some measure of power.

Being naturally moved to rejoicing by this narrow escape, I wrote "The Yellow Wallpaper," with its embellishments and additions, to carry out the ideal (I never had hallucinations or objections to my mural decorations) and sent a copy to the physician who so nearly drove me mad. He never acknowledged it.

The little book is valued by alienists and as a good specimen of one kind of literature. It has, to my knowledge, saved one woman from a similar fate—so terrifying her family that they let her out into normal activity and she recovered.

But the best result is this. Many years later I was told that the great specialist had admitted to friends of his that he had altered his treatment of neurasthenia since reading "The Yellow Wallpaper."

It was not intended to drive people crazy, but to save people from being driven crazy, and it worked.

ELAINE R. HEDGES

Scudder's Comment on
"The Yellow Wallpaper"*
(1973)

It wasn't easy for Charlotte Perkins Gilman to get her story published. She sent it first to William Dean Howells, and he, responding to at least some of its power and authenticity, recommended it to Horace Scudder, editor of *The Atlantic Monthly,* then the most prestigious magazine in the United States. Scudder rejected the story, according to Gilman's account in her autobiography, with a curt note:

> "Dear Madam,
>   Mr. Howells has handed me this story. I could not forgive myself if
> I made others as miserable as I have made myself!
>   Sincerely yours,
>   H. E. Scudder"

In the 1890s editors, and especially Scudder, still officially adhered to a canon of "moral uplift" in literature, and Gilman's story, with its heroine reduced at the end to the level of a groveling animal, scarcely fitted the prescribed formula. One wonders, however, whether hints of the story's attack

---

* Excerpted for fair use in the classroom from *The Yellow Wallpaper.* Brooklyn: The Feminist Press, 1973.

on social mores—specifically on the ideal of the submissive wife—came through to Scudder and unsettled him?

The story was finally published, in May 1892, in *The New England Magazine*, where it was greeted with strong but mixed feelings. Gilman was warned that such stories were "perilous stuff," which should not be printed because of the threat they posed to the relatives of such "deranged" persons as the heroines.

SANDRA M. GILBERT
AND SUSAN GUBAR

From The Madwoman in the Attic: The Woman Writer and the Nineteenth-Century Literary Imagination
(1984)

As if to comment on the unity of all these points—on, that is, the anxiety-inducing connections between what women writers tend to see as their parallel confinements in texts, houses, and maternal female bodies—Charlotte Perkins Gilman brought them all together in 1890 in a striking story of female confinement and escape, a paradigmatic tale which (like *Jane Eyre*) seems to tell *the* story that all literary women would tell if they could speak their "speechless woe." "The Yellow Wallpaper," which Gilman herself called "a description of a case of nervous breakdown," recounts in the first person the experiences of a woman who is evidently suffering from a severe postpartum psychosis. Her husband, a censorious and paternalistic physician, is treating her according to methods by which S. Weir Mitchell, a famous "nerve specialist," treated Gilman herself for a similar problem. He has confined her to a large garret room in an "ancestral hall" he has rented, and he has forbidden her to touch pen to paper until she is well again, for he feels, says the narrator, "that with my imaginative power and habit of story-making, a nervous weakness like mine is sure to lead to all manner of excited fancies, and that I ought to use my will and good sense to check the tendency" (15–16).

The cure, of course, is worse than the disease, for the sick woman's mental condition deteriorates rapidly. "I think sometimes that if I were only well enough to write a little it would relieve the press of ideas and rest me," she remarks, but literally confined in a room she thinks is a one-time nursery because it has "rings and things" in the walls she is literally locked away from creativity. The "rings and things," although reminiscent of children's gymnastic equipment, are really the paraphernalia of confinement, like the gate at the head of the stairs, instruments that definitely indicate her imprisonment. Even more tormenting, however, is the room's wallpaper: a sulphurous yellow paper, torn off in spots, and patterned with "lame uncertain curves" that "plunge off at outrageous angles" and "destroy themselves in unheard of contradictions." Ancient, smoldering, "unclean" as the oppressive structures of the society in which she finds herself, this paper surrounds the narrator like an inexplicable text, censorious and overwhelming as her physician husband, haunting as the "hereditary estate" in which she is trying to survive. Inevitably she studies its suicidal implications—and inevitably, because of her "imaginative power and habit of story-making," she revises it, projecting her own passion for escape into its otherwise incomprehensible hieroglyphics. "This wallpaper," she decides, at a key point in her story,

> has a kind of sub-pattern in a different shade, a particularly irritating one, for you can only see it in certain lights, and not clearly then.
> But in the places where it isn't faded and where the sun is just so—I can see a strange, provoking, formless sort of figure, that seems to skulk about behind that silly and conspicuous front design. (80)

As time passes, this figure concealed behind what corresponds (in terms of what we have been discussing) to the facade of the patriarchal text becomes clearer and clearer. By moonlight the pattern of the wallpaper "becomes bars! The outside pattern I mean, and the woman behind it is as plain as can be." And eventually, as the narrator sinks more deeply into what the world calls madness, the terrifying implications of both the paper and the figure imprisoned behind the paper begin to permeate—that is, to *haunt*—the rented ancestral mansion in which she and her husband are immured. The "yellow smell" of the paper "creeps all over the house," drenching every room in its subtle aroma of decay. And the woman creeps too—through the house, in the house, and out of the house, in the garden and "on that long road under the trees." Sometimes, indeed, the narrator confesses, "I think there are a great many women" both behind the paper and creeping in the garden,

> and sometimes only one, and she crawls around fast, and her crawling shakes [the paper] all over. . . . And she is all the time trying to climb through. But

nobody could climb through that pattern—it strangles so; I think that is why it has so many heads. (190)

Eventually it becomes obvious to both reader and narrator that the figure creeping through and behind the wallpaper is both the narrator and the narrator's double. By the end of the story, moreover, the narrator has enabled this double to escape from her textual/architectural confinement: "I pulled and she shook, I shook and she pulled, and before morning we had peeled off yards of that paper." Is the message of the tale's conclusion mere madness? Certainly the righteous Doctor John—whose name links him to the anti-hero of Charlotte Brontë's *Villette*—has been temporarily defeated, or at least momentarily stunned. "Now why should that man have fainted?" the narrator ironically asks as she creeps around her attic. But John's unmasculine swoon of surprise is the least of the triumphs Gilman imagines for her madwoman. More significant are the madwoman's own imaginings and creations, mirages of health and freedom with which her author endows her like a fairy godmother showering gold on a sleeping heroine. The woman from behind the wallpaper creeps away, for instance, creeps fast and far on the long road, in broad daylight. "I have watched her sometimes away off in the open country," says the narrator, "creeping as fast as a cloud shadow in a high wind."

Indistinct and yet rapid, barely perceptible but inexorable, the progress of that cloud shadow is not unlike the progress of nineteenth-century literary women out of the texts defined by patriarchal poetics into the open spaces of their own authority. That such an escape from the numb world behind the patterned walls of the text was a flight from dis-ease into health was quite clear to Gilman herself. When "The Yellow Wallpaper" was published she sent it to Weir Mitchell, whose strictures had kept her from attempting the pen during her own breakdown, thereby aggravating her illness, and she was delighted to learn, years later, that "he had changed his treatment of nervous prostration since reading" her story. "If that is a fact," she declared, "I have not lived in vain." Because she was a rebellious feminist besides being a medical iconoclast, we can be sure that Gilman did not think of this triumph of hers in narrowly therapeutic terms. Because she knew, with Emily Dickinson, that "Infection in the sentence breeds," she knew that the cure for female despair must be spiritual as well as physical, aesthetic as well as social. What "The Yellow Wallpaper" shows she knew, too, is that even when a supposedly "mad" woman has been sentenced to imprisonment in the "infected" house of her own body, she may discover that, as Sylvia Plath was to put it seventy years later, she has "a self to recover, a queen."

ANN J. LANE

From To Herland and Beyond: The Life and Works of Charlotte Perkins Gilman
(1990)

So common were debilitating diseases of the nerves among women in Victorian America that one inevitably seeks clues hidden in the collective life of the nineteenth century. The frustrations many were forced to accept in a society that denied them any but the most limited range of options provided the battleground on which psychological and related physical ailments were fought.

The traditional manner in which people had previously lived was being smashed as capitalism in America moved into its industrial stage in mid-century. Women's lives were recreated, as were men's, but differently. The world was rapidly ending in which husband and wife shared a life of agricultural production, working at different jobs, but with the recognition of the essential interdependence of their labor. Production was moving out of the home, forcing men to follow, seeking work in the new public arena of factory and office. Women stayed behind; even those who worked outside the home generally felt their primary identification was tied to it and that their work in the public sphere would end with eventual marriage and children.

Among the working-class population, single women went off to work in factories or in private homes as domestic servants; married women earned money by taking in boarders, washing the clothes of the wealthy, or doing piecework sewing at home, and in general providing substantial economic value to their homes in various forms of unpaid labor. Middle-class and upper-class women found themselves locked into their homes, rather than driven out of them. They became "hostages to their homes," in Barbara Welter's words, caretakers of home, husband, and children, the anchor upon whose "voluntary" self-sacrifice the stability of the social order came to rest. The talents and skills of these women were not permitted to share in the production of goods or services required by the society at large. Their work was to minister to their private families. Not all women suffered in these circumstances; many accepted their life and enjoyed it, not finding its restrictions oppressive or suffocating. But rigid notions of proper behavior and activity for women denied the rights of many others whose needs and desires did not fit the ideal and who were granted no alternative. It is true that, as we have seen, increasing numbers of women sought alternative ways to shape their lives, but the total number of such women remained small.

The problem for women who were not comfortable with the prevailing ideal of femininity was that it not only defined options concerning activities and behavior but presumed also to take charge of women's psychological needs. The ideal woman was not only assigned a social role that locked her into her home, but she was also expected to like it, to be cheerful and gay, smiling and good-humored. Because myths that permeated the lives of most women told them both what they were supposed to do and what they were supposed to feel, it was difficult for women to acknowledge negative feelings about their prescribed role.

The outcome of being confined to such an explosive, closed psychological state was predictable: numbers of women struggled, often unsuccessfully, with intense inner turmoil and accelerating internal tension. Ambitious and imaginative women who found themselves with no outlets for their abilities, while in the larger culture opportunities proliferated for ambitious and imaginative men, suffered particularly.

Diaries, letters, and medical case studies detail the range of diseases that devastated numbers of women in the middle and upper classes from the antebellum period through the turn of the century. Descriptions of depression, spiritlessness, exhaustion, and hysteria fill the writings of many such women and their doctors. "I sometimes . . . wonder that I am alive," sadly wrote one, whose overpowering sense of futility and joylessness was shared by so many others.

In a world that admonished women to retain an exemplary pose of permanent cheer, one could credit such depression as a form of rebellion, but if so, the rebellion damaged the rebel most seriously. For it came out of unexpressed anger, unfulfilled emotional needs, and unexamined feelings of guilt and inadequacy at not fulfilling the role that was being rejected.

Men, too, suffered similarly, for they were as rigidly locked into social roles and behavior as women, though of a different sort. Men too broke down, many of them, perhaps as many as women; we have no way of being certain. We need not look further than Charlotte's own Beecher kin, beginning with the patriarch Lyman Beecher, who apparently suffered from what today would be called manic-depressive illness. He often fell into long periods of apathy and depression, or "the hypo" (hypochondria), as depression was then designated. At other times he displayed extraordinary energy, what seemed to others superhuman vitality. When on the verge of nervous and physical collapse, as he was periodically throughout his life, he threw himself into exhausting physical work, if he could. He used parallel bars and other gymnastic equipment in his backyard, and when the weather was too bad for outdoor activity, he shoveled sand from one side of his cellar to the other and back again. Earlier he had used farm labor to deal with his tendency to depression.

Many of his children suffered similarly. Mary, "the Lady," Charlotte's grandmother, the one who accepted her domestic role, was one of the few exceptions among the thirteen. James, the youngest, with a history of violence, suffered like his father from manic-depressive states, had a severe breakdown, and spent four years at Dr. Gleason's water-cure sanitarium before he shot himself. Thomas, again like his father, experienced enormous mood swings that went from exuberance to depression. Catharine suffered a severe breakdown in 1829 at the age of twenty-nine, and another in 1835. Years later, in an address to a graduating class, she described the experience as one where she "found the entire fountain of nervous energy exhausted . . . utter and irretrievable prostration. . . . I could not read a page or write a line, or even listen to conversation without distress." (Her great-niece was to write startlingly similar descriptions of herself years later.) For more than ten years Catharine went regularly to a sanitarium where she was treated with waters from a mineral spring thought to have healing qualities. She also underwent hypnosis to relieve pain she felt had psychological origins.

Harriet, too, suffered some form of serious depression in her early twenties. She described it as being caused by the "constant habits of self-government which the rigid forms of our society demand. . . . My mind is exhausted and seems to be sinking into deadness," she wrote to a woman friend in 1832, when she was twenty-three years old. Another breakdown occurred when she was in her late thirties, leaving her feeble for a year and fearing permanent invalidism. After spending seven months in the same sanitarium where Catharine had stayed, Harriet returned home substantially improved. Only much later did she find real release in her writing. Although her brood of children continued to increase, she began writing furiously at night and discovered that she suffered no ill effects, physical or emotional. "In fact," her biographer says, "her health was better than it had been at any time since childhood," although it was only with the financial success of *Uncle Tom's Cabin* that she was able to relieve herself of the domestic responsibilities that were so burdensome.

I have dwelt upon the emotional history of Charlotte's famous Beecher relatives, not because the family was unique in its psychiatric background, but because it was not. Not *all* families were filled with members who regularly broke down, of course, but the phenomenon was common enough in middle- and upper-class households. We know more about the famous families because they are famous and probably not primarily because they were more prone to collapse, although the ambition that made them famous likely contributed to the strain that caused the collapse.

In the mid-1840s persons suffering from nervous diseases took the waters, as did Lyman Beecher's family. The drank and bathed in mineral springs that were naturally saline and contained calcium chloride and that were believed to cure a range of ailments from gout and rheumatism to anemia and liver problems. Whatever limitations were intrinsic to the water cure, it provided a place of rest and removal, if only temporarily, from the world's tensions. It also offered the presence of a largely female supportive community, since most of those who sought relief were women. The water cure was certainly preferable to leeches or drugs, both of which were common medical alternatives.

Although the water cure continued to be popular through the 1890s, later in the century other kinds of treatment began to appear for women's nervous diseases. There was, for instance, the Adams Nervine Asylum, founded in 1877 to treat nervous people who were not psychotic. The institution had facilities for thirty patients, all women, and provided, as did the water cure, prolonged rest and absence of responsibility. Other efforts at dealing with ailing women patients utilized the "Swedish movements," a set of exercises, or motorpathy, a kind of massage. Often used in conjunction with massage, or by itself, was the application of electric current to various parts of the body on the assumption, referred to as the theory of "galvanism," that there was a similarity between electrical and nervous power or energy. Medical practice rested on the belief that all mental disorders could be traced to diseases of the nervous system, as nerves were seen as the link between mind and body. Thus doctors could treat the presumed physical disorder to get at the mental one. Some doctors had their own theories about the cause of nervous diseases. Others had no idea what caused them, and simply experimented with a variety of techniques that would at least alleviate some of the symptoms and might offer some clue about their origin.

Men and women tried a variety of cures, some for both genders and some for only one. The choice of cure depended in part on the class to which they belonged and, therefore, the funds that were available. All of the cures were geared to preparing the patient to return to his or her place, men to men's work, women to women's work. The distribution of the work itself by sex seems never to have been questioned.

Charlotte Stetson's confrontation with the renowned and respected neurologist Dr. Silas Weir Mitchell was a crucial moment in her life, a moment she used to begin her liberation. At the time of their meeting, Mitchell was at the height of his powers and she was at her lowest.

Even before his new patient arrived at his sanitarium just outside Philadelphia, Mitchell had formed certain assumptions about her. He found utterly useless the long letter she had written to him detailing her symptoms; that she should imagine her observations would be of any interest to him was but an indication of her "self-conceit," he advised her. He had already treated two Beecher women; "two women of your blood" was the way he put it. It was a bad start.

What manner of man did Charlotte Stetson encounter when she entered Mitchell's well-appointed office? He was a handsome, vigorous, urbane, self-confident man in his mid-forties, who that very year had been granted an honorary degree, his first of many, from Harvard University, and who was then elected to the presidency of the Philadelphia College of Physicians.

As a young man, just after his medical training, Mitchell had turned to the study of rattlesnake venom and related nerve injuries. During the Civil War that interest came to focus on human paralysis caused by wounds and bites, and this led him thereafter to an interest in paralysis that developed in the absence of any recognizable physical cause, and in the end to his lifelong work at the "boundary between physiology and psychology." Mitchell remained a neurologist, that is, a "nerve doctor," who tried to cure patients who suffered from motor and sensory malfunctioning.

At the time Mitchell met Charlotte Stetson, he had an international reputation as a neurologist and as a research scientist who had made original contributions to the study of poisons and nerve diseases, although his reputation was greatest as a specialist in the nervous diseases of women. He had an enormously affluent medical practice. He was adored and venerated by hundreds of women patients who traveled from all over the world to undergo his treatment.

Mitchell had also begun publishing novels and poetry, and although at this time his major energies were engaged by his work as a pioneer psychologist and neurologist, toward the end of the century his literary work became his prime occupation. By the time of his death he was a prolific and immensely popular writer, not only of hundreds of articles and several books on medicine but also of some twelve novels, a controversial biography of George Washington (his unfavorable portrayal of Washington's mother as overbearing caused a stir), many successful children's stories, one of which went through twelve editions, and several volumes of verse.

A man of extraordinary versatility, he was viewed, and not just by Philadelphians, as a contemporary Ben Franklin. He was the father of two sons, both of whom achieved distinction in their own work. He married twice, his first wife dying young, and both marriages appear to have been successful. He was thought to be a genius, "an opinion Mitchell came to share," as one of his biographers put it. If he was not a genius, as subsequent generations have come to acknowledge, he was indeed a formidable and overwhelming presence for a frightened and fragile Charlotte to face.

But he had not always been so self-assured. He had himself evolved from an emotional state startlingly close to that which he treated in his patients. Emotional traumas he had suffered early in his life and the control he achieved over them were at the root of the growing and seemingly flawless successes he went on to achieve in his maturity. He chose to work in the very area—nervous diseases—in which he had himself suffered as a young man. Weir Mitchell, son of an affluent Virginia doctor, described his early life as repressed, dominated by an extraordinary father for whom he had, he said, "a sort of veneration" and a mother for whom he felt "a passionate love." His father initially opposed his decision to become a doctor, saying he was "wanting in nearly all the qualities that go to make success in medicine." Weir persisted, and his father relented, but then insisted he become a surgeon. "Surgery was horrible to me," Weir admitted, but he went on to become a surgeon. He soon found it impossible to continue because he fainted regularly and developed a tremor in his hand. Unable to refuse his father's command, he seems to have developed physical disabilities that made surgery impossible. He did as a young man what Charlotte Stetson did as a young woman: he and she made it impossible to do what they did not want to do.

When the Civil War broke out he was appointed head of a hospital that handled nerve wounds and diseases, a splendid professional opportunity to establish a speciality that eventually made him famous. After the war he suffered the loss of wife and father, which set off a nervous breakdown. He went to Europe for a two-month recovery period. Three years later, in 1872, his mother died, and he suffered another breakdown. Then he married for a second time and thereby stepped from the gentry into the aristocracy of Philadelphia. Mary Cadwalader Mitchell devoted her impressive personal skills and family connections to providing a good home for him. From this time on "the sunshine of life," as a biographer said, began to shine on this previously depressed and unhappy man, and his enormously successful career began.

In her interviews with Mitchell, Charlotte Stetson was told she was suffering from neurasthenia, or exhaustion of the nerves, a disease that was commonly held to be associated with the pressures of nineteenth-century American society. It was, in the words of another renowned doctor treating the illness, a "neurosis without organic basis." Neurasthenia, said George M. Beard, one of the most respected physicians of the period, is "impoverishment of nervous force." At the time it was popularly compared to an overloaded electrical current and an overdrawn bank account, observes a twentieth-century historian of medicine. Most physicians of the period believed that each person possessed a certain amount of nervous energy, which was transmitted to different parts of the body. Neurasthenia was a result of a breakdown in the system, of the demand exceeding the supply. When the limited quantity of nervous energy was improperly used, there was, in the words of one neurologist of the time, a "partial or general nervous inefficiency, or perversion, of the nerves," affecting particular organs, different in men and women.

Although many men were diagnosed as suffering from neurasthenia, Silas Weir Mitchell's attention was primarily addressed to its manifestation in women. In fact, one might say he moved from treating one marginal group, wounded men, to another precarious group, vulnerable women, that he spent his life testing his manhood as an endless demonstration that he could match his father's success. As a doctor, Silas Weir Mitchell sought groups to minister to who helped him define his own maleness. By controlling women patients who were weak and helpless, perhaps he could purge himself of those remaining fears of female weakness that had tied him to his revered mother.

In 1871 Mitchell examined neurasthenia in his book *Wear and Tear.* Three years later he wrote *Nurse and Patient* and *Camp Cure* on the same subject. He became famous for the treatment he developed and called the Rest Cure. During the 1870s he published an analysis and description of various aspects of his Rest Cure in several medical journal articles, but in 1877 it had its fullest examination in his little book *Fat and Blood.* Neurasthenia was developed, he argued, by the "wear and tear" of our overcivilized life. The foundation of his medical treatment was to improve nutrition and to restore energy by revitalizing the patient. He evolved rather than discovered the treatment, he said, by combining several standard medical procedures already in fashion.

The treatment subjected the patient to: 1) extended and total bed rest; 2) isolation from family and familiar surroundings; 3) overfeeding, especially with cream, on the assumption that increased body volume created new energy; 4) massage and often the use of electricity for "muscular excitation" to compensate for the passive regimen to which the body was limited.

The purpose of the isolation from friends and family was to disrupt old habits and cut off hurtful influences, but above all, Mitchell said, to separate "the invalid from some willing slave, a mother or a sister." Isolated from the familiar, the patient was subject to total enforced rest. Mitchell's idea was to enforce that rest and isolation so severely that the patient was "surfeited with it and welcomed a firm order to do the things she once felt she could not do."

In Mitchell's view this treatment constituted "moral medication," necessary because women suffering from these diseases were, he felt, characterized by a kind of "moral degradation." They had "lost the healthy mastery which every human being should retain over her emotions and wants." He also referred repeatedly in his writings to "the selfishness which a life of invalidism is apt to bring about." "If you tell the patient she is basely selfish she is probably amazed and wonders at your cruelty. To cure the case you must morally alter as well as physically amend, and nothing else will answer." This "moral medication" commanded his women patients, Charlotte Stetson among them, to return to the work of women: care of home, husband, child.

Fat and Blood included detailed descriptions of the treatment and its effect on many women patients. The Rest Cure was not designed, said its creator, to satisfy "these thin-blooded emotional women, for whom a state of weak health has become a long and almost, I might say, a cherished habit." A patient was restricted to bed, where initially she was not permitted to read, write, sew, converse, or feed herself. One nurse cared for her during her stay, which might last from six weeks to two months. At the beginning of the treatment the patient was forbidden to use her hands at all except to brush her teeth, nor was she allowed to move out of her bed or even in it by herself. The process of infantilization was presumed to "make the patients contented and tractable"—tractable like docile children, in the view of one modern critic.

Enforced rest, enforced passivity, acceptance of the commands of male authority: Mitchell's treatment was an extreme version of the cultural norms that operated outside his sanitarium, just as, ironically, the incapacity of these women patients took the form of an exaggeration of the very qualities they had been taught to value.

Mitchell could not imagine a woman like Charlotte Stetson and therefore could not treat her properly. Able to see only what he was trained to see, as most of us are, he saw a woman shirking her duty and determined to get her back to it.

A few years before he met Charlotte Stetson he described hysteria "among women of the upper classes . . . caused by unhappy love affairs, losses of money, and the daily fret and weariness of lives, which passing out of maidenhood, lack those distinct purposes and aims which, in the lives of men, are like the steadying influences of the fly-wheel in an engine." That a woman's life might have a "distinct purpose" like that which informed "the lives of men" was apparently beyond him. A rigid personality kept Mitchell from any imaginative leap beyond the norms of his culture; even in his later years, when the world had somewhat altered, Mitchell could not accommodate to change in customs or values.

In addressing Radcliffe's student body in 1890, he expressed his view that women in general often collapsed under the strain that higher education imposed on their physical and emotional state. "I no more want [women] to be preachers, lawyers, or platform orators, than I want men to be seamstresses or nurses of children," he told the women undergraduates. His notion of a proper education was one that taught child care and domestic skills. Mitchell objected to any girl under the age of seventeen using her brain even moderately. To do so, he warned, would endanger her health, and her future would be "the shawl and the sofa." Although there were many women and some men in 1890 who challenged the validity and sense of separate spheres for men and women, Mitchell was not among them.

The writer Owen Wister, an old and dear friend, described how Mitchell, to his death in 1914, "obstinately clung to his own view of traditional women. . . . The truth was his standard was extremely conventional; his ideal woman was the well-sheltered woman. . . . So those who loved him felt it wise to turn the conversation whenever it drifted dangerously in the direction of the New World."

Mitchell's restrictive notion of proper womanhood, and the dangerous result his treatment might and did have on many women, still should not obscure the positive value of certain aspects of his Rest Cure. Its goal was to permit neurotics to function normally, and in order to accomplish such a goal, Mitchell had to assume that neuroses were treatable and curable and that the gulf between normal and abnormal behavior did not permanently divide people as was widely believed at the time. If he was not the first to "take psychiatry out of the madhouse [and bring] it into everyday life," he surely made an important contribution to that process. He took seriously the complaints of his patients. He knew their suffering was real, and he focused on relief. Cure was to be sought by a natural approach to medical practice, and Mitchell's practices have a ring of something that would today be called holistic medicine, for he was careful to stress the entire person, not one diseased portion.

The torment that Charlotte Stetson suffered for years was made worse by the well-meant but damaging responses of loved friends and family.

She herself could not understand why a healthy, energetic woman collapsed without cause—she never did understand—and surely those around her did not understand and therefore, however much they tried, could not genuinely sympathize with or comprehend her pain. Their wonderment, which always ended in gently urging her to try just once more, only made her more clearly aware that it was somehow her lack of will, her lack of character, that had permitted her to behave in a fashion often described as "lazy." Weir Mitchell told her she was not "lazy," she was sick. She was sick, but she could be well if, under his guidance, she created an atmosphere in which she could regain her health through her own efforts.

For many patients, the psychological value of receiving attention and acknowledgment that the ailment was legitimate in an environment that encouraged self-confidence was sufficient to restore some semblance of normal functioning. Mitchell's treatment did seem to "work" a good deal of the time, if the number of satisfied patients is evidence. An uncritical biographer maintains that "there is no doubt that Dr. Mitchell did not expect and did not forgive failure. Success might take a long time but come it *must*, otherwise he lost interest."

Not just many women patients and their families but Freud as well was impressed with Mitchell's technique, stating that he was adding his own psychoanalytic therapy to "the Weir Mitchell rest cure." Freud reviewed *Fat and Blood* and described Mitchell as the "highly original nerve specialist in Philadelphia." Years later, in 1895, in *Studies on Hysteria*, Freud again referred favorably to Mitchell and to the Rest Cure.

Weir Mitchell—and Charlotte Stetson—lived in a world that had not yet learned to think psychologically, and it is very difficult for us today to recreate such a world. They had to seek motivation and understanding in the upper reaches of consciousness. Changes in behavior were sought as a product of retraining such as Mitchell attempted in his Rest Cure, retraining aimed at restoring to the enervated woman a sense of her capacity and a belief in her power to exert her will. Mitchell saw himself as permeating the listless bodies of his women patients and instilling them with his strength, releasing his power into them. Gilman later used the image of a muscle, relying as she always did on the physical body for strength, literally and metaphorically. The brain was a muscle, and emotions were a form of muscle; the more one flexed them and used them, the more control one achieved over them. Mitchell used an early form of behavior modification, a retooling of patients' skills to restore to them lost powers.

The idea of the unconscious that Freud later introduced, and particularly his emphasis on sexuality, were anathema to both Mitchell and Gilman, one of their few strongly shared beliefs. In the treatment of his patients, Mitchell showed no particular interest in sexual matters, and indeed rarely referred to sexuality at all in his writings on nervous diseases. One of the few references was to the danger of sexual excess, rather than of repression, as a contributing factor to some nervous diseases. "Where did this filthy thing come from?" was Mitchell's response to the first, and probably last, book of Freud's he perused, just before he threw it in the fire. Mitchell, and most of his colleagues who practiced therapy, rejected the new psychoanalytic doctrines of Freud as they were expounded by his followers in England and America. To have acknowledged the social and moral implications of Freudian doctrine would have required a profound revision in the values they had upheld their entire lives. In any case, at the time of Charlotte Stetson's treatment by Mitchell, Freud had not done his significant work.

Very little is known about the actual treatment Charlotte received in Mitchell's Philadelphia sanitarium. The final entry in her diary in 1887 was written in April, just before she set off to see Mitchell. In her autobiography, she said she was put to bed in the sanitarium and kept there. "I was fed, bathed, rubbed. . . . After a month of this agreeable treatment, he sent me home."

Consistent with his conventional views of woman's role, Mitchell could in good conscience send Charlotte Stetson home with these instructions after pronouncing her "cured":

> Live as domestic a life as possible. Have your child with you all the time. . . .
> Lie down an hour after each meal. Have but two hours' intellectual life a day.
> And never touch pen, brush or pencil as long as you live.

This advice, which Charlotte quotes in her autobiography, was offered to a woman who was trained as a commercial artist and who was beginning to forge a career as a writer. And the consequences?

> I went home, followed those directions rigidly for months, and came perilously near to losing my mind.

Her description of the subsequent months makes it clear that she was indeed "perilously near to losing" her mind. "I made a rag baby," she said, "hung it on a doorknob and played with it. I would crawl into remote closets and under beds—to hide from the grinding pressure of that profound distress."

Finally, in the fall of 1887, the unhappy couple agreed to separate— Walter very reluctantly—although they did in fact live together for another year before they were able fully to accept this decision. In September 1888, Charlotte, with barely any money, with no marketable skills with which to earn a living, in a mental state still not far from collapse, took her baby Katharine and went back to California, not to San Francisco where her father lived, but to Pasadena, to the warmth of the sun and to the warmth of the Channings. Walter followed the next year, hoping their life together was not over, but the reconciliation failed. Legal complications kept their divorce from becoming a reality for a long time, but with her flight to California—and it can only be seen as the desperate escape of a desperate woman—Charlotte Stetson began a new phase of her life.

"I decided to cast off Dr. Mitchell bodily, and do exactly what I pleased," wrote Charlotte to a friend in November 1887. And she did; from that moment on she patterned a life for herself that repudiated his explicit instructions to her. Charlotte Stetson's rejection of a seemingly loving and loved husband and of the country's leading neurologist constitutes the first major act of defiance in her entire life, defiance against the accepted rules of her world, rules that determined how one behaved and to whom one deferred, rules that were imposed upon her with difficulty but that she nevertheless had accepted as her own.

As we have seen, Charlotte had expended enormous amounts of energy trying to do what was expected of her, first by her mother, then by her husband, and finally by her doctor. Now, for the first time, she was truly declaring her independence.

She struck for freedom when she fled from Weir Mitchell and Walter Stetson, but she had not the habit of introspection nor any respect for the value of wallowing in the deep recesses of one's mind, and so she never achieved much understanding of the tensions that led to her collapse. Even at the end of her life she continued to ask, as she did in her autobiography, "What is the psychology of it?" Admitting in her autobiography that "part of the ruin" was a product of her childhood, part was a result of her "rigid stoicism," but most was caused by her marriage, she asserted that had she enjoyed a "period of care and rest" in 1890, after she was "free," she might have made a full recovery and not suffered periodic nervous collapses and depressions all her life. The solution she wished she could have sought was an entirely physical one—rest. These prescriptions from the perspective of her later years ran directly counter to what she actually did at the time: rejected orders to rest and stay passive and instead moved out on her own, taking responsibility for herself, asserting her sense of self against doctor, husband, mother, and, eventually, child. In fact, her observation that had she had a "period of care and rest" after her flight to Pasadena she might have made a fully recovery is a sentiment that strangely echoes Mitchell's Rest Cure idea. She was free, but not entirely.

The struggle between Charlotte and Weir Mitchell also occurred in a literary arena. Neither one was known primarily as a writer of fiction, but both used that genre to examine characters and situations that came from their personal psychological experience. Charlotte wrote more than half-a-dozen novels and hundreds of short stories, but the one piece of fiction that stands as a brilliant psychological study is her most famous, "The Yellow Wallpaper," which she wrote in Pasadena in 1890 and which was published in the May 1891 issue of *New England Magazine.* In it, she critically portrays a Rest Cure similar to Mitchell's, and implicitly recommends a very different approach, thus, in effect, usurping the place of her former doctor.

In 1913 Gilman included in the *Forerunner* a brief statement entitled "Why I Wrote 'The Yellow Wallpaper.'" That statement and a few relevant pages in her autobiography published more than twenty years later represent her entire public expression on the matter of Mitchell. "For many years I suffered from a severe and continuous nervous breakdown tending to melancholia—and beyond," she said in 1913, probably the first time she made such a public admission. After suffering for about three years, she consulted, "in devout faith and some faint stir of hope," a noted specialist in nervous diseases (who remained unnamed). His advice, which she followed for three months after returning home, brought her "so near the borderline of utter mental ruin that I could see over." Casting aside his orders, and with the help "of a wise friend," she resumed work—"work, the normal life of every human being; work, which is joy and growth and service, without which one is a pauper and a parasite."

She was so "naturally moved to rejoicing by this narrow escape" that she decided to tell her story, but with a different end. The story describes, she said, the "inevitable result" of her doctor's treatment for those who stay with it, and that is "progressive insanity." She wrote the piece, she said, "to save people from being driven crazy."

"The Yellow Wallpaper" is a study of a young mother's descent into madness, caused by a well-meaning but insidious husband–doctor who follows S. Weir Mitchell's Rest Cure. In the story John, the husband, takes his ailing wife, who is suffering from a nervous disease, to the country for the summer, along with their baby and the nurse.

John, as husband–doctor, embodies Mitchell's treatment, but he lacks the neurologist's major strength of acknowledging the legitimacy and seriousness of his patient's illness.

John is a physician, and *perhaps* (I would not say it to a living soul, of course, but this is dead paper and a great relief to my mind)—*perhaps* that is one reason I do not get well faster.

You see, he does not believe I am sick! And what can one do?

Her husband is not alone in asserting that she is not really ill. Her brother, also a physician, confirms the diagnosis.

John rents a large, isolated, run-down home (analogous to his wife's psychological state of isolation and disintegration) to provide his ailing wife with "perfect rest." And so they move to "the nursery at the top of the house," a literal acting out of the infantilizing process. She had preferred a room downstairs, one that opened onto a piazza, but John pointed out that there was "not room for two beds and no near room for him if he took another." Thus her preference was for a room leading out, an escape, and a room without space for her loving, adoring John. In the converted nursery, the bed is nailed down and there are bars on the window. There is no escape. John's treatment has a reminiscent ring:

So I take phosphates or phosphites—whichever it is—and tonics, and air and exercise, and journeys, and am absolutely forbidden to "work" until I am well again.

Personally I disagree with their ideas.

Personally, I believe that congenial work, with excitement and change, would do me good.

But what is one to do?

The young wife accepts the definition of herself as others see her. When John leaves "a schedule prescription for each hour in the day," she comments, "he takes all care from me, and so I feel basely ungrateful not to value it more." She observes that she gets "unreasonably angry with John sometimes," and maintains that "it is due to this nervous condition." She tells us that John "is very careful and loving, and hardly lets me stir without special direction"—language remarkably similar to that which Charlotte Stetson used to describe Walter.

She persists in believing that if she only could "write a little it would relieve the press of ideas and rest me," but she finds herself as the weeks go on, too tired to write in secret and forbidden to write publicly.

John ultimately threatens her. If she does not get well faster she shall be sent to Weir Mitchell, and she is terrified of going. She had a friend "who was in his hands once," and "she says he is just like John and my brother, only more so!" This is the only reference to Mitchell by name in the story. He is cast as someone even more dangerous than her husband, whom by now we recognize as the force leading her to her destruction. John calls her "his darling and his comfort and all he had," but he will not listen to her pleadings that he take her away. She is his "little girl," and he exerts the power of father, husband, and doctor combined. "I am a doctor, dear, and I know," he tells her.

As her condition deteriorates, the woman becomes obsessed with and increasingly disgusted by the yellow wallpaper in her bedroom. It has no predictable pattern. When she tries to follow the "lame uncertain curves" in the paper, "they suddenly commit suicide." Within the wallpaper there is a 'strange, provoking, formless sort of figure that seems to skulk about," an ambiguous form that threatens, frightens by its skulking. As the days pass, the shape gets clearer. "And it is like a woman stooping down and creeping about behind the pattern." It is frightening that she wishes to escape, but John, who is so wise and loves her so, will not acknowledge her need. At night the pattern in the paper becomes clearly bars, like the bars on the windows, and the woman in the wallpaper becomes plainly visible, imprisoned behind the bars at night, just as the young woman imagining her feels imprisoned, just as the author who created the young woman used to feel imprisoned. The figure begins to "shake the pattern, just as if she wanted to get out." Nighttime, of course, is also the time when John is present, in the great immovable bed that is nailed down.

The young wife now wants John in another room because he is so odd. She also wishes to keep for herself the secret of the woman in the wall coming out at night. John, she now believes, only pretends to be loving and kind.

As the story nears its grim conclusion, the young woman, in an effort to escape the barred windows, tries to move the bed, but it will not move; she has forgotten that the bed is nailed. She gets so angry that she bites a piece off one corner, hurting her teeth. She is now like the ravaging children who gnawed at the bedstead long before she occupied it. She is both child and mother. She is the child in the mother. Frantically she peels off the paper and sees "all those strangled heads and bulbous eyes and waddling fungus growths," imagery which brings to mind dead babies. She contemplates suicide, but decides it would be wrong and, in any case, confined as she is, impossible.

The remaining escape is another route to self-destruction. It is madness. She is now surrounded by creeping women, and she is one of them, but unlike the others, she will not stop her creeping at night to crawl back into the wall. And all this while John is at the door calling for an axe to break it down. She stops his forcible entry with her madness, for he enters the room and faints. She escapes by creeping over him.

"The Yellow Wallpaper" is an intensely personal examination of Gilman's private nightmare. Never again in her writing did she take such an emotional chance or engage in such introspection as she did in this story. After writing it, Charlotte did not for many years return to fiction, except for an occasional effort at collaboration with Grace Channing in writing drawing-room comedies. Perhaps the emotional truth and intensity of "The Yellow Wallpaper" drained her; perhaps it frightened her.

"The Yellow Wallpaper" thus stands apart from the entire body of her extensive fiction. It is, in my opinion, the only genuinely literary piece she ever created and it is also, of all her fiction, the most clearly, the most consciously autobiographical.

When Charlotte said that she wrote the piece to "save people from being driven crazy," perhaps one of the people she saved was herself, for in this story she seems to have let herself go, allowed her unconscious to help her creative art, and in so doing may have helped to purge the demons that terrified her. Although she cited a didactic reason for writing it, "The Yellow Wallpaper" is not a simple product of ideology, as most of her other fiction is. She did not just write about what she knew, using her experience to provide her with material, as Mitchell did. She used her experience to plumb her inner life by conjuring up the past and using it to help others through her words, and in so doing she achieved some control over both her illness and her past.

Charlotte permitted herself to touch emotions and dredge up deep-hidden fears in this semi-autobiographical, fictionalized story in ways she could not in her autobiography, in her letters, in her diaries, or in her time of treatment with Mitchell. The language and the imagery she used in the story allowed her to express buried fears, fear of her own baby, memories of childhood's blank walls, walls that did not encompass mother-love or father-love, fears of being strangled, devoured, violated by those who pretend to love and by those whom one is supposed to love and protect.

She recreated nightmares of her own childhood in which she is the child abandoned by a rejecting mother and an absent father. The young mother in the story has abandoned her baby to another, as Mary Perkins abandoned Charlotte by withholding needed expressions of love, and as Frederick literally abandoned her. The young mother in the story is imprisoned in the nursery, where she becomes a baby and recreates over and over again horrible, fantastic nightmares in which she faces the terror of all babies, dead or alive, and all mothers who deny and push away, just as the mother of little Charlotte pushed away her hand when it sought her mother's cheek.

The scarred and thwarted psyche of Charlotte Perkins, suffering from the fears that haunt an abandoned child, was driven further into trauma by a cultural voice, Walter Stetson's voice and particularly Silas Weir Mitchell's voice, commanding that she not seek relief in work; that she imprison herself everlastingly with a child whose terrifying demands she felt she could never satisfy; that she abide by a Victorian morality that denied her, as it had denied her mother, avenues to express feelings of rage and hostility; that she achieve mastery of self and womanly restraint but without being permitted to develop the tools and resources to achieve that mastery. Although Charlotte never explained to her own satisfaction the causes of her breakdown, in "The Yellow Wallpaper" she makes clear the context in which the mental collapse took form. She, Charlotte Stetson, found relief by externalizing, by writing about and creating a fictional person who, finding her desire to write aborted, went mad.

One suspects that "The Yellow Wallpaper," the work of fiction, is closer to the truth than Charlotte's seemingly accurate autobiography. For whatever reason, Charlotte publicly sustained a heroic vision of Walter Stetson. A few slightly bitter diary entries aside, Walter Stetson is consistently drawn in saintly terms. In her autobiography she speaks of his "unbroken devotion, his manifold cares and labors in tending a sick wife, his adoring pride in the best of babies." In a diary entry from 1884, written as "the gray fog drifted across my mind" she said: "He has worked for me and for us both, waited on me in every tenderest way, played to me, read to me, done all for me as he always does. God be thanked for my husband."

Why, then, if God is to be thanked for Walter, did she make John, the husband in "The Yellow Wallpaper," the villain? Is that the thanks Walter gets? Or is some kind of quasi-conscious anger finally surfacing, if only in fictional form? Charlotte describes in "The Yellow Wallpaper" how at night, dangerous night, the imprisoned figure creeps about in "that undulating wallpaper." And the yellow, the smoldering, repellent yellow, developes a smell as well. The woman in the story wakes up at night "to find it hanging over me." It is, she says, "the most enduring odor I ever met," and perhaps it is, even if Gilman did not recognize it, the dreaded smell of sex, a sensual smell, excretion of the night. The woman lies on her "great immovable bed—it is nailed down." John, the "loving" husband, imprisons her in a room with no escape, with bars on the windows, in a bed nailed down, trapped with a child, for the foul smell is also a smell, perhaps, of a child's feces, and the yellow wallpaper also embodies fear of babies. The woman sees a recurrent spot where "the pattern lolls like a broken neck and two bulbous eyes stare at you upside down." The spot becomes "impertinent," an odd word to use of a design. She gets angry with its impertinence and its "everlastingness," and what new mother has not felt some resentment at the "everlastingness" of the demands of a tiny infant?

The designs crawl sideways with those "absurd unblinking eyes," a familiar view to a mother nursing a child. "I never saw so much expression in an inanimate thing before, and we all know how much expression they have!"—though it is not clear who the "they" are supposed to be—inanimate, sleeping babies, who sleep like the dead, and then instantly are awake, crying, demanding, asserting their wants? She continues: "I used to lie awake as a child," entertained and terrorized by blank walls and plain furniture. The woman sees frightening images of babies in the walls and immediately thinks, not of her baby on the floor below, but of herself as a child. The images are of a baby, the one she has and never sees, and the one she was, and she is frightened by them. It is her own baby and herself as baby that terrify her, perhaps pregnancy as a threat to the life of the mother, perhaps the insatiable needs of children that devour their mothers and from which mothers must protect themselves by withdrawing from their children, Mary Fitch Perkins from Charlotte, Charlotte Perkins Stetson from Katharine, the young woman in the story from her baby, both unnamed. Later in the story, when the wallpaper begins to move, the woman locked inside shakes the paper, anxious to get out, but she is in danger of being strangled by the many heads, upside down, with white eyes—again the image of babies strangling, devouring their mothers.

The children in the nursery have, at some time in the past, before memory, torn the room apart. It looks "as if it had been through the wars." The narrator says she "never saw such ravages as the children have made here," an acknowledgment of the damage that children can do, the power they have to destroy. "How those children did tear about here! This bedstead is fairly gnawed." Children again are likened to dangerous animals that tear and destroy.

The young wife, locked upstairs in the hideous room, has one comfort: "The baby is well and happy, and does not have to occupy this nursery with the horrid wallpaper." The mother has sacrificed for her baby, and the sacrifice will cost her her sanity; babies, and their insatiable needs, drive their mothers mad.

"The Yellow Wallpaper," was originally seen as a horror story. It has been reprinted as a horror story. Although it got its first feminist reading from Elaine R. Hedges in the Feminist Press edition of 1973 and has since won recognition as something of a feminist classic, awareness of its feminist dimension should supplement, not replace, an appreciation of its power as a story of horror. When it originally appeared, it elicited a good deal of response of all kinds. For example, an unnamed doctor published a letter arguing that the story could hardly "give pleasure to any reader," and indeed "must bring the keenest pain" to those whose lives have been touched "by this dread disease." For others, "whose lives have become a struggle against an heredity of mental derangement, such literature contains deadly peril," and one wonders, the good doctor concluded, whether "such stories [should] be allowed to pass without severest censure."

After "The Yellow Wallpaper" appeared, Charlotte received a good deal of mail, much of it favorable, including a lengthy, congratulatory letter from a physician. Until "The Yellow Wallpaper," he said, "there has been no detailed account of incipient insanity." Presenting himself as a former opium addict who inspired trust in a drug-addict patient because, as the patient said, "Doctor, you've been there!" he asked of Charlotte a similar revelation: "Have you ever been—er—; but of course you haven't." She replied that she "had been as far as one could go and get back."

Charlotte Stetson's description of her collapse is the description of a woman who hit bottom: holding a rag doll and weeping, sitting on the floor, being a baby rather than caring for one. In this state she accepted Silas Weir Mitchell's treatment. Mitchell became another version of a commanding, authoritative father-figure but at least he was what a father-figure was conventionally supposed to be, at any rate in relation to his patients. With Mitchell, Charlotte finally got the attention she wanted from a father, and perhaps she was thus able to engage that male power, reject it, and move out on her own.

Frederick Douglass wrote in his autobiography how when he had a bad master he wanted a good master, but when he had a kind master he was able to see that he wanted none at all. A childhood spent deprived of both mother-love and father-love leads the child, whatever her age, to seek, desperately seek, parental engagement. When some authority in the clear role of an authoritative and authoritarian father intercedes, issues orders, commands, takes charge, then there is a force, a negative force, against which to rebel, a tyranny to reject. Freud's talking therapy later was to stress the value of free association and resistance in the treatment of neuroses. "The Yellow Wallpaper" was Charlotte's version of free association, a controlled version, and her rejection of Silas Weir Mitchell's power over her life is somewhat comparable to the crucial resistance in a therapeutic setting. She had transferred her need for a father to her doctor, rejected the father by rejecting the substitute, and then took an additional step by talking it out.

Perhaps Weir Mitchell's ultimate contribution to Charlotte Stetson was that he allowed her to deny her father's power sufficiently to begin to heal herself. With her break from Weir Mitchell, and soon thereafter a break from Walter Stetson, Charlotte Anna Perkins Stetson began to build her life again.

MARY A. HILL

From Charlotte Perkins Gilman:
The Making of a Radical Feminist
1860–1896
(1980)

On Friday, May 2nd, 1884, Charlotte put the finishing touches on her wedding dress, trimmed her bonnet, arranged "great stacks of flowers," and then flew about nervously trying to seem calm. At about 6:30 that evening, she and Walter Stetson were married, his father, Joshua Stetson, presiding. "Aunt C[aroline] was hearty in her congratulations," and Walter's "parents were kind and affectionate, but Mother declines to kiss me and merely says 'good bye.'" Charlotte continued in her diary:

> I install Walter in the parlor and dining room while I retire to the bed-chamber and finish its decoration. The bed looks like a fairy bower with lace, white silk, and flowers. Make myself a crown of white roses. Wash again, and put on a thin drift of white mull fastened with a rosebud. He meets me joyfully; we promise to be true to each other; and he puts on the ring and the crown. Then he lifts the crown, loosens the snood, unfastens the girdle, and then—and then.
>
> O my God! I thank thee for this heavenly happiness! O make me one with thy great life that I may best fulfill my duties to my love! to my Husband!
>
> And if I am a mother—let it be according to thy will!
>
> O guide me! Teach me, help me to do right!

The next day she wrote:

> Up at 8:20 or so. Get a nice little breakfast of omelette and chocolate. Lie on the lounge in the soft spring sunshine and am happy, Happy, Happy. Walter stays quietly at home with me; and we rest and love each other. Get johnny-cakes and frizzled beef for dinner; wash dishes, Walter wiping; . . . put my boy to bed, (he is well worn out with a long winter's work,) . . . O I am happy! May I do right enough to merit and deserve!
>
> *Thank God*

Charlotte and Walter had planned only a short weekend honeymoon at home. They lounged about, read together, arranged things in their new apartment, trying awkwardly, self-consciously, to create an atmosphere of wedded bliss. Charlotte's way was to tackle kitchen duties and to loaf (though neither was her style). On Sunday she washed dishes and made bread while Walter read to her. On Monday, the honeymoon over, she fixed an elaborate breakfast, napped three hours while Walter worked, and made dinner when he came home at two. "Then loaf a bit, wash dishes and fix bedroom. He feels dizzy, and I put him snugly to bed and then write. Am happy."

The next week was more or less the same. She shopped, called on friends, lazed about, and tried to teach herself to cook. (Her mother had done most of it at home.) Tuesday she made a "most delectable dinner of veal fried in batter and new potatoes. Very very delicious," she wrote. "Am tired later and am put tenderly to bed." But she was "turning out [to be] a superior cook," she decided, and was pleased that Walter noticed.

For all her earlier jibes against domestic work—she had told Martha it was an insufferable bore—Charlotte now seemed to think not only that love meant giving, but that woman's love meant cleaning, cooking, and managing the housework. Being a man, Walter had other kinds of work to do; in fact, marriage added further purpose to his public, professional commitment. He had no time or energy, inclination or know-how to concern himself with pots and pans, mops and brooms and such. That was Charlotte's province. There was one day (or one moment of one day) back in 1882 when he had thought differently. Aware of her keen ambitions, but unaware of practicalities, he had written, "I hereby take my solemn oath that I shall never in future years expect of my wife any culinary or housekeeping proficiency." But if promises came easy, they faded from his memory when he faced the reality which (as Charlotte later remarked) very quickly and "rudely breaks in upon love's young dream. On the economic side, apart from all the sweetness and truth of the sex-relation, the woman in marrying becomes the house-servant, or at least the housekeeper, of the man." Spontaneously, only one week after their wedding, Charlotte wrote in her diary: "I suggest he pay me for my services; and he much dislikes the idea. I am grieved at offending him, mutual misery. Bed and cry."

Several weeks later, she got a letter from her brother Thomas that probably helped matters not at all (from Walter's point of view). Thomas wrote, "Realizing the great need of all young married people—the need of a quantity of advice and instruction of sundry and various kinds—I take great pleasure herewith transmitting a sufficient quantity thereof to not only supply your own needs, but peradventure several generations of your predecessors."

Then, as though he knew precisely what was at issue, he "continued continuously thereon and thereafter" and proceeded to sketch a broom on one side of the page and Webster's unabridged dictionary on the other. The first was "woman's alleged sceptre," the second "Woman's (real) sceptre," he quipped. "Either may be construed in several ways. You can suit your own taste. *Mine* is to consider one to typify cleanliness and the other conversational ability—some would suggest force of arms and fluency of invective."

Walter may have been concerned or irritated, but in either case he was not dumb. In fact, he seemed quite supportive. For example, he began reading the story of Atalanta's race "for" her. And when she faced a "vast accumulation of dishes," wisely he came home and helped. Actually, Walter assumed a lot of household chores, though in part it was because Charlotte complained so much of feeling tired and sickly. "Bed. Am disgusted with myself—numb—helpless," Charlotte wrote after several weeks of marriage. "Tomorrow God helping me I will begin anew!"

Charlotte sometimes found that intellectual activity helped to boost her spirits, so she began reading again, talking "earnestly" with friends "on foreordination and free will," and studying "obstetrics diligently." But for the most part she seemed absorbed with housework, physical ailments, and Walter's kind attentiveness. July 3: "Scrub out house and stairs. . . . Go over to Mother's, darn stockings and talk." June 13: "Feel sick and remain so all day." June 14: "Walter gets breakfast. . . . Walter helps much. . . . Read and eat candy while Walter draws me in bed. Am happy."

But the next day, and in the days that followed, Charlotte felt differently: "Am sad: last night and this morning. Because I find myself too—affectionately expressive. I must keep more to myself and be asked—not borne with." June 25: "Get miserable over my old woe—conviction of being too outwardly expressive of affection." June 26: "still miserable and feel tired. . . . Am miserable some more but he persuades me to believe that he never tires of me."

These were remarkable statements for a nineteenth-century bride to have made—sensuous, even demanding, though apologetic. At least Charlotte was *trying* to adhere to appropriate "true womanhood" ideals of virtue and purity. But if some healthy gusty inclinations sometimes interfered, she piously and consciously tried suppressing them. "Purity," she believed, "is that state in which no evil impulse, no base thought can come in; or if forced in dies of shame in the white light. Purity may be gained by persistent and long continued refusal to entertain low ideas." Since Walter had probably worked long and hard to exercise restraint as well (sexual repression was not confined to women, after all), there must have been debilitating, irksome strains in their relationship—a sense of awkwardness, repulsion, fear—all well-supported by "Victorian" strictures concerning the sinfulness of sex.

For many nineteenth-century couples, the marriage adjustment must have been a rough one. For Charlotte, it was probably rough enough to intensify depressions she was feeling anyway, or at least so her later published writings would suggest. "One of the most pitiful errors of our views on this matter," she later asserted, "is letting young girls enter this relationship without a clear understanding of what they are undertaking." "Gaily to the gate of marriage they go, and through it—and never have they asked or answered the questions upon which the whole truth of their union depends." That was to become one of Charlotte's passionate convictions: a woman has the need for and right to a fulfilling love relationship, not love as the be-all and end-all of her life, but as a vital and critically important part of it. Charlotte may not have held such views before her marriage, nor may she have asked "questions upon which the whole truth" of a love relationship depends. But her diary entries only weeks following her wedding, her oblique references to thwarted passion, her mounting discontent and illness suggest a vague fear of being trapped in marriage without the satisfying experience of love.

In any case, whatever the fears or disappointments, an already difficult situation soon was exacerbated, perhaps irreversibly, by the fact that Charlotte became pregnant. On August 3 she wrote, "feel sick all day." August 8: "Sick still. . . . I eat, but lo! it remaineth not within me but returneth to upper air." Her mother brought flowers—"Dear kind thoughtful little woman!"—helped clean the house, washed the dishes, talked and tried to cheer her up. And Walter intensified his domestic efforts too, preparing meals, shopping, cleaning, comforting for hours. Walter was patience and tenderness personified (or so Charlotte recalled); but he also was undoubtedly somewhat piqued by what seemed to him to be irrational, even irresponsible behavior—"hysterical" crying fits, interminable doldrums, unreasonable demands. To him, firmness and masculine assertiveness seemed appropriate when feminine emotionality got out of hand. "Dismal evening," Charlotte wrote, "for I feel unable to do anything and am mortally tired of doing nothing. Get out on roof. Humbly ask if I can sleep there tonight and am told 'No you cannot!' Serves me right for asking. Bed? I guess so." Fortunately, her mother came and comforted her with pears and flowers.

Mary must have felt some rather intense anxieties, as well as conflicting loyalties, as she worried over Charlotte's pregnancy. Her own had been so frightful, so nearly fatal. (If Mary shared her pregnancy images and recollections, that, by itself, could have generated a good deal of Charlotte's dread.)

But to make matters worse, Thomas wrote saying he needed Mary's help. He had been living in the West for years, had a wife and child, and was making an urgent appeal on the basis of his family's health. Of course Mary felt compelled to go, despite her apprehensions over Charlotte. And if Charlotte managed to encourage Mary's trip, she also felt disappointed, perhaps even abandoned, at just the time she especially wanted Mary's warmth. On September 18, Charlotte wrote, "I go up to mother's for the last time." And three days later: "sicker than I've been since any part of it. Walter . . . does everything."

For the next several months, in fact for the entire fall and winter that Mary was gone, Walter served as nursemaid, and Charlotte withdrew into a kind of self-denying lethargy. For the most part, she even put aside her diary-writing, summarizing, at the year's end, her mood of "happy" wifely acquiescence:

> My journal has been long neglected by reason of ill health. I am now better, and hope to keep it regularly and to some purpose. . . . [Walter] has worked for me and for us both, waited on me in every tenderest way, played to me, read to me, done all for me as he always does. God be thanked for my husband! . . .
>
> This last year has been short. I have done little, read little, written little, felt and thought—little to what I should have. I am a happy wife. I bear a child. I have been far from well . . . perhaps humbler. Ambition sleeps. I make no motion but just live. And I am Happy? Every day almost finds me saying so, and truly. And yet—and yet—"call no man happy until he is dead." . . . I should not be afraid to die now, but should hate to leave my own happiness and cause fierce pain. Yes I am happy.

January through March 1885 were months of continuing illness and depression. Only occasionally did she feel much spunk. She played chess from time to time, ran errands (somehow she remembered Walter's birthday), sewed sheets and baby clothes, and wrote letters to her mother. She also read some, notably the forthright woman's paper *Alpha*, but wrote very little. Mostly she was ill. January 15: "I get so tremulous and teary that my boy stays with me." January 29: "very hot and nervous evening. . . . [Walter] puts me to bed in a blanket." January 30: "Bed in blanket. Get frantically hot and nervous and kick out of it. Bad night, lame all over." February 2: "I *must* be strong and not hinder him. . . . Feel so downcast that I take out my comforter, Walter's journal, and get new strength and courage thence, learning how good and brave he is."* February 4: "Am very very tired and lame at night which displeaseth and grieveth my Walter. I didn't *mean* to!" February 17: "So hysterical indeed that Walter decides to stay with me." February 19: "A wellnigh sleepless night. Hot, cold, hot; restless nervous hysterical. Walter is love and patience personified; gets up over and over."

Katharine Beecher Stetson was born on March 23, 1885. Charlotte noted the event in her diary.

> This day, at about five minutes
> to nine in the morning, was born
> my child, Katharine.
>
> Brief ecstasy. Long Pain.
> Then years of joy again.
>
> Motherhood means—Giving.

If motherhood meant giving, it meant dependency as well, a sense of childlike vulnerability which Charlotte could neither control nor understand. Nancy Chodorow suggests such feelings are rather common: "The experience of mothering for a woman involves a double identification. A woman identifies with her own mother and, through identification with her child, she (re)experiences herself as cared for child." Chodorow believes that pregnancy and childbirth are almost inevitably threatening to a woman's sense of self, a "challenge to the boundaries of her body ego ('me'/'not-me' in relation to her blood or milk, to a man who penetrates her, to a child once part of her body)." Since mothering so often involves "the excitation of long-buried feelings about one's own mother," Charlotte may have experienced what one writer described quite incisively: "as a mother suddenly I found myself a child again."

For the first two months after Katharine's birth, Mary stayed with Thomas, and Charlotte had a nurse to help, but was still "pretty well used up by the loss of sleep"—the lament of new parents almost everywhere. "I wonder what people do who know even less than we do about babies! And what women do whose husbands are less sufficient." Yet even with Walter's support, Charlotte felt irritated, cheerless, weepy—an exasperating contrast to romanticized wife and mother expectations she had sometimes harbored.

---

* Walter Stetson's journal may still be among the rich collection of family papers owned by the Chamberlin family, but at the time this was written, it was not available for research.

May 2: "The first anniversary of my wedding day. I am tired with long sleeplessness and disappointed at being unable to celebrate the day. So I cry . . . dress myself in black silk, jersey, and yellow crepe neckerchief. Haven't been 'dressed' in months."

Two days later she received a telegram from her mother: "She starts [home] today. I shall be glad to see her!" Charlotte had kept Mary informed about her pregnancy, Katharine's birth, and various discouragements and ailments. Now she seemed more than willing to let Mary take control. On her mother's first visit after arriving in Providence, Charlotte wrote: "am very tired and depressed in the morning. . . . At about noon mother comes, bless her, and thereafter all goes well. She worships the baby of course; and to my great relief and joy declares her perfectly well. We have a happy afternoon." For the next several weeks, Mary came almost every day—relieving tensions, taking charge of Katharine, managing the house while Charlotte rested and gratefully observed. In fact, this was one of the few times that Charlotte expressed (in her diary anyway) some real appreciation for her mother: "Mother over early. She takes all the care of the baby day times; washes her today with infinite delight." "So nice to have mother here."

Mary doubtless remembered enough of her own tear-filled frustrating times with babies not only to work calmly and efficiently, but also to help Charlotte dispel some guilt-producing illusions about mothering, and learn some hard-headed survival tools instead. In ways not possible during more rebellious years, Charlotte may have felt much stronger mother-daughter bonds with Mary. Some were negative, of course—bonds based on mutual suffering, on learning to accept the disappointments of being a wife and mother. But others were more positive—bonds based on practical assistance, on mutual emotional support, on tenderness. In fact, the example of Mary's strength and the gift of Mary's love may have been Charlotte's major comfort.

At the time, however, it did not always seem that way. The more generous Mary was, the more guilty Charlotte seemed to feel for disappointing her, for complaining, for not adapting smoothly. Mary seemed patient and giving (Charlotte forgot that Mary had not always seemed that way), Charlotte mean and selfish by comparison. Yet there were some other dynamics operating too, more rebellious ones, which were temporarily obscured. For if at times Charlotte viewed Mary as a model she should emulate, at other times Mary was the exemplar of "virtues" Charlotte almost spontaneously abhorred. For years, Charlotte had described the "warring elements" within herself—"feminine" domestic instincts fighting "masculine" ambitious ones. Now she faced a major showdown, a consummation of her self-fulfilling prophecy of misery: "Here was a charming home; a loving and devoted husband; an exquisite baby, healthy, intelligent and good; a highly competent mother to run things; a wholly satisfactory servant—and I lay all day on the lounge and cried." "Motherhood means giving," she simplistically assumed; yet nothing "was more utterly bitter than this, that even motherhood brought no joy." "I would hold her close—that lovely child!—and instead of love and happiness, feel only pain. The tears ran down my breast."

In part then, it may have been a condemnation of domestic virtues, as well as a condemnation of herself for not possessing them, which so intensified Charlotte's misery during the first few years of marriage. She thought anger or resentment of mothering responsibilities was inappropriate, unjustified, the opposite of mother-love. But since anger and resentment kept cropping up even as she tried to squelch them, at times she lost her self-control. Gradually (but not consistently), she became what one writer has called a "paragon of Victorian femininity"—"helpless, housebound, and ineffectual." As she put it in her diary when Katharine was five months old, "Every morning the same hopeless waking . . . the same weary drag. To die mere cowardice. Retreat impossible, escape impossible." She may have found it easier to explain the crisis to Martha than to Walter, but in effect she made a desperate appeal to both: "I let Walter read a letter to Martha in which I tell my grief as strongly as I can.* He offers to let me go free, he would be everything in the world for me; but he cannot see how irrevocably bound I am, for life, for life. No, unless he die and the baby die, or he change or I change, there is no way out. Well."

Crises, quarrels, and crying spells followed, the diaries chronicling complaint after miserable complaint. September 14: "Cry more after breakfast. An oppressive pain that sees no outlet." September 25: "Dreary days these. Only feel well about half an hour in all day." These were months of severe "hysteria," perhaps temporary "insanity" as well.

> I could not read nor write nor paint nor sew nor talk nor listen to talking, nor anything. I lay on that lounge and wept all day. The tears ran down into my ears on either side. I went to bed crying, woke in the night crying, sat on the edge of the bed in the morning and cried—from sheer continuous pain. Not physical, the doctors examined me and found nothing the matter.

---

* The letter, written in August 1885, is not in the Martha Luther collection, and may not have been preserved. In any case, Martha's response did not seem very helpful. Charlotte's diary reads: "I wrote her my heart and she answers with not overwise head" (Diary of Charlotte Perkins Gilman, Sept. 5, 1885, AESL).

One of Charlotte's major lifelong complaints was that no one realized how sick she was. No one sympathized enough. Little was known about mental illness in the 1880s, she explained, and many "openly scoffed" at her tears and "laziness." "Earnest friends" suggested that she use her will power, but from her point of view she "had used it, hard and long, perhaps too hard and long; at any rate it wouldn't work now." People did not seem to understand that her "mind was exclusively occupied with unpleasant things." Still, while Charlotte insisted that quips and scorns of friends and relatives had exacerbated her sense of failure, she also willingly acknowledged that the blame heaped on her by others could not match the blame she heaped upon herself. Her autobiography suggests that she never fully overcame her sense of guilt. "Eight years of honest conscientious noble-purposed effort lost, with the willpower that made it. The bitterness of that shame will not bear reviving even now."

> Feeling the sensation fear, the mind suggests every possible calamity; the sensation shame—remorse—and one remembers every mistake and misdeed of a lifetime, and grovels to the earth in abasement.

> . . . Prominent among the tumbling suggestions of a suffering brain was the thought, "You did it yourself! You did it yourself! You had health and strength and hope and glorious work before you—and you threw it away. You were called to serve humanity, and you cannot serve yourself. No good as a wife, no good as a mother, no good at anything. And you did it yourself!"

But while Charlotte carefully recorded anger with herself, what she failed to note in her autobiography was that she had blamed Walter too and that she had by no means lost her ability to say so—indirectly, but publicly and well. For despite her illness, she prepared an article for publication, entitled "On Advertising for Marriage," that was printed in *Alpha* in September 1885.

The major theme of the article is that men irresponsibly and far too rapidly push women into marriage. Men are attracted by women's femininity and charm, but care not a whit for their real personalities and concerns. Men pursue, flatter, and then propose, Charlotte wrote, without having "genuine sympathy and appreciation"—not of her "sexual nature! Heaven defend us! [Men] have studied that long and well, but the *rest* of her, the 'ninety-nine parts human!'" Charlotte seemed to feel that "beauty of the body and its sexual attraction" had inspired Walter's passion, but that her complex character was well beyond his ken.

If a man sees a fair woman before he knows her; feels the charm of her presence before he begins to understand her character; is first aroused to the necessity of judging by his strong inclination; surely he stands less chance of a cool and safe decision than one who begins knowingly, learns a character from earnest letters, loves the mind before he does the body. And that first love would improve and be more to him yearly, growing ever richer, stronger, and more lovely with advancing age.

Charlotte's self-styled therapy, then, was to analyze the faults and foibles of her marriage, and to direct some of her energy and roaring anger into arguments which left self-respect intact. Her article was an attack on Walter (without saying so, of course). He had proposed seventeen days after their first meeting, had pursued her persistently thereafter, and had never come to know her for who she really was.

In part that was true, though there was another side as well. Surely one reason Walter failed to understand her, though admittedly he did not take much time to try, was that she had such difficulty being honest and direct. Only in the first few months after she met him did she openly reveal her complexities and contradictions. Thereafter, her letters were deferential and uncharacteristically sweet. She apologized, kept her peace when issues bothered her, and, at least, tried to display "feminine" humility instead. In short, by attempting to be gentle and submissive and loving according to prevalent "feminine" ideals, by trying to outgrow "devil's daughter" fractiousness and become a "lady," she had disguised herself, as women so often do, and then blamed Walter for misunderstanding her.

●   ●   ●

By autumn 1885, Charlotte and Walter had reached an impasse. Unhappiness and irritation led to attack and counter-attack, then to screaming arguments, crying fits, and "hysteria." Grace Channing offered Charlotte a temporary respite by inviting her to spend the winter with the Channing family in Pasadena, California. The Channings had moved there when tuberculosis threatened Grace's health, and, under the circumstances, a trip West seemed to offer prospects of relief for Charlotte's "illness" too: "We propound discuss and decide the question of shall I travel? Yes, I shall. . . . Hope dawns. To come back well!" So with mother and a maid left in charge of her baby and the house, and armed with "tonics and sedatives," Charlotte set off alone to cross the continent.

First, she visited her brother in Ogden, Utah, obviously not too sick for some prankish retributive horseplay. She decided to surprise him: "He came to the door in his shirt-sleeves, as was the local custom, holding a lamp in his hand. There stood the sister he had not seen in eight years, calmly smiling. 'Good evening,' said I with equanimity. This he repeated, nodding his head fatuously, 'Good evening! Good evening! Good evening!' It was a complete success."*

Thomas had gone West in the fall of 1879 to work as a mining engineer first in Nevada, and then in Utah. In his own way, he may have been rebelling also—against the straight-laced New England relatives or some not-so-straight ones, against the demands, accusations, or perhaps self-fulfilling prophecies of his mother; probably he was rebelling against Charlotte too, since from his perspective she was the successful one, the family dynamo. In any case, he had quit school (involuntarily), moved from job to job, settled in a mining town in Utah, and proceeded to become the strange hybrid, a New England–born-and-bred, rough, tough Westerner.

If Charlotte was impressed, perhaps she was envious as well, tasting a bit of raucous frontier living, and contrasting it to her own domestic hell. To make matters worse, but a lot more fun, Thomas gloated in ways designed to shock. For instance, he took her to a dance at the town hotel in order to show her examplars of the local culture: one man had killed someone, he proudly noted, but people did not seem to care; another man "had been scalped three times—the white patches were visible among the hair"; still others, whom Thomas inveigled to play whist, were tobacco-chewing swashbuckler types whose frequent use of the cuspidor rather challenged Charlotte's pseudo-prim repose.

From Utah, Charlotte went to San Francisco to pay a visit on her father, whom she had not seen, in fact probably had not heard from, for several years. Like Thomas, Frederick moved around a lot, and just recently he had accepted a position as head of the San Francisco Public Library. To some extent, Charlotte still unconsciously viewed him as her mentor, her masculine ally as she faced the "warring elements" within herself—mind versus emotion, ambition versus commitment to one's family—those vaguely defined dichotomies she assumed were tangling up her life. Since she may have felt that Frederick had rejected emotional involvement because of his ambitions, because he preferred public work to private disruptions, perhaps she thought he would appreciate her conflicts as well. But Frederick's choices had been different, his attitudes conventional: For one thing, child care and domesticity were not a male's concern; and for another, he rather liked

---

* It had been six years since Charlotte had seen Thomas, not eight as she remembered.

the double-standard image of the loving-serving wife. Quite likely then, Frederick did not offer Charlotte the advice or affection, and most certainly not the collusive sympathy, that she craved. For whatever he said, whatever his response to her chronicle of troubles, she later could recall only his cold indifference and her own all-too-familiar disappointment. She wrote, father "took me across to a room he had engaged for me for a day or two. Here he solemnly called on me, as would any acquaintance." Then, as though to prove she had not wanted his affection anyway, she politely told him, "'If you ever come to Providence again I hope you will come to see me.' . . . To which he courteously replied, 'Thank you. I will bear your invitation in mind.'"

From San Francisco, Charlotte then went to Pasadena. The flowers were "a-glory," she later wrote, the Arroyo Seco "wild and clean." "The vivid beauty of the land, its tumultuous growth of flowers and fruit, the shining glory of the days and nights, gave me happiness and health." "Callas bloomed by the hydrant, and sweet alyssum ran wild in the grass. Never before had my passion for beauty been satisfied. This place did not seem like earth, it was paradise." Health and stamina seemed to be returning.

> Kind and congenial friends, pleasant society, amusement, outdoor sports, the blessed mountains, the long, unbroken sweep of the valley, with snow-peaks at the far eastern end—with such surroundings I recovered so fast, to outward appearance at least, that I was taken for a vigorous young girl. Hope came back, love came back, I was eager to get home to husband and child, life was bright again.

That was Charlotte's autobiographical reflection, but her first letter to Martha Lane during the winter visit was a bit more qualified: "I have not written to you for so long because of—circumstances. The mere writing itself is still an effort; and then my mental condition has made me oblivious of even my best friends. In despair of ever getting well at home I suddenly undertook this journey. It has already done me an immense amount of good, and I expect to return in the spring as well as I ever shall be. Perhaps that is not saying much."

This letter was written in early January 1886. Charlotte had been in Pasadena only a few weeks, Christmas celebrations were barely over, and the noise and stir alone had been enough to wear her out. Still she was optimistic. The Channings "are all very kind to me," she wrote, "and I gain rapidly." She described her enjoyment of the mountains, valleys, and plains, the flowers, fruits, and foliage. And lightly, momentarily, she expressed some feelings of affection for her daughter too, as though thinking about Martha's child, Chester, helped her love her own: "I wish he was near enough for me to see more of him, for I know he is just the child I should love and enjoy. Dear bright little face! It makes me homesick for my own baby." (Charlotte's sense of pain and guilt were so intense that the statement has a certain poignancy despite its cliché sentimental cast.)

Charlotte's visit with the Channing family was just what a perceptive doctor might have prescribed. Rigorous conversationalists and intellectuals, supportive and congenial friends, the Channings welcomed Charlotte almost as a family member. They helped her forget domestic responsibilities, stop her introspective worries, and be more accepting of herself. Grace's father, Dr. William F. Channing, was the leading spirit of the group. He was a writer, a medical doctor, a geological surveyor, a former abolitionist, an active social reformer, and a co-inventor of the telephone, for which Alexander Graham Bell had gotten all the credit. Moreover, he had provided the stimulation, if not the direct encouragement, necessary for his daughter Grace to grow up thinking that women could be doers and achievers too.

Grace Channing had been one of Charlotte's favorite friends in Providence. An avid reader, a generous confidante, Grace was also an aspiring novelist and poet, one of the few "thinking companions" who shared some of Charlotte's literary goals. But if there were many things the two women had in common, there were substantial differences as well. Grace was often weak and sickly, Charlotte was the physical fitness enthusiast; Grace was more self-effacing and quiet, more "delicate, shrinking, and spirituelle," whereas Charlotte (by nature anyway) was more raucous and aggressive. If Grace was (as one literary critic put it) "like some fine plant of the north flowering amidst the riotous hues of the south yet in consonance with it," Charlotte was more like the Arizona cactus, beautiful and flowering at times, but also prickling, towering, and, some would have argued, overbold. Grace, then, was the "womanly woman," the champion of women's long-suffering, self-sacrificing beauty, their nobility in face of illness, poverty, and death.* Charlotte usually preferred the fighting, rebellious kind of woman.

---

* See particularly Grace Channing's *Sister of a Saint and Other Stories.* The beautiful martyrdom of Grace's heroines may have reflected goals she adopted for herself. When, several years later she found herself (her own illnesses notwithstanding) caring not only for a husband, a child, and a house, but also for two invalid and ailing parents, she wrote to her father-in-law: "But I do firmly believe the German saying: 'Out of Love can man do all things.' I am trusting my strength will last so long as my father or mother need me. After that I will make it last for Walter's sake!" (Grace Channing to Joshua Stetson, Dec. 22, 1896, BL). That was Walter Stetson she was referring to, to move the story ahead. Following Charlotte's divorce in 1894, Grace and Walter were married.

Or, to put it in male terms, Charlotte preferred a Julius Caesar-type martyr to a Christ-like one.

But whatever the differences of style or fantasy or personality, Charlotte and Grace put their heads together that winter of 1885–86 and began improvising plays. They started out just spoofing and bantering with one another, then reshaping and practicing the lines, then writing out the dialogue, recruiting friends, and producing amateur, but quite successful, shows. Charlotte was ecstatic. She wrote to Martha Lane: "You can see I am not so sick as I was. . . . O but twas fun! To write a play and give it ourselves, all in a real theater, to a real audience, who laughed and clapped and enjoyed it. We enjoyed it more. It's a pretty good play. We're going to try and sell it."

Momentarily elated with success, Charlotte proceeded to review her winter's progress rather optimistically: "Have painted a very little here, learned much, made a few friends, gained what I came for—health, and written a Play!" But her concluding comments were rather sombre: "My California winter is about done. Shall start for home in a week or two more. I look forward with both joy and dread. Joy to see my darlings again, and dread of further illness under family cares. Well. I have chosen."

●   ●   ●

After returning to Providence in the spring of 1886, Charlotte wrote in her diary, "Am trying to get accustomed to life here. It will take some time." Katharine seemed to be her major worry. "Baby exasperating about her nap." Or, "Manage to paint two sheets of notepaper under great disadvantage from Miss Katharine." Charlotte occasionally enjoyed some playful romping with the child. But when she also wanted to think, paint, write, or be alone, toddler Kate would still be going strong—playing, laughing, fussing, screaming—Charlotte fuming in dismay. Walter helped a lot with child care, but tensions mounted: "Do not feel well during the day. . . . Get hysterical in the evening while putting K. to sleep. Walter finishes the undertaking and sleeps with her. When I am nervous she never does sleep easily—what wonder." Again and again Charlotte recorded that "Dear Walter" had given patient cooperative assistance; but she also noted there was "always the pain underneath," always an awkward resistance as she tried to say "I love you" to her "Dear Tender Heart."

While Charlotte appreciated Walter's help, she sometimes resented his independence more. It would be hard to guess how many hours she and Walter shared child-care duties, and how many hours she stayed alone with Kate. But very likely, as the breadwinner and the male, Walter spent most days painting at his studio, though he helped Charlotte when he could. Charlotte, by contrast, spent most days caring for Katharine and doing housework, though she wrote or painted when she could. Walter liked his professional responsibilities, and was relatively calm and confident. Charlotte hated her domestic work, was frustrated and ambivalent, and cried a lot. At times she tried to feel the appreciation she thought a wife and mother ought to feel, but at other times she expressed resentments fully, or so her fiction suggests. For it was about this time, the fall of 1886, that she wrote a little fiction piece, entitled "Allegory," that could easily be viewed not only as an attack on the inequalities of marriage, but also as a hate-filled blast at Walter.

"Allegory" describes a lifelong power struggle between two brothers—unequal from the start. The stronger despised the weaker, "made a mould for his brother and kept him in it," and then flaunted his own superiority: "'I am strong and thou art small.' And the weaker brother bore it, for he loved him well." The stronger gained experience and know-how in sports and warfare, wrote "great books," grew "exceedingly wise" and virtuous, and then ridiculed his imprisoned brother for being cowardly, ignorant, and bad. At times the weaker brother started to resist, but since the stronger "laughed at him and cursed him . . . he came back and re-entered the mould; for he loved him well." Finally, the weaker grew despite himself: "the mould broke continually, . . . in the end it broke utterly, so that he could bear it no more." The stronger "lifted his hand against him in deadly warfare, and the end thereof who can tell?"

That was just what the situation with Walter had come to, "deadly warfare" with terrifying consequences. "Hysterical" at times, Charlotte was a verbal virtuoso at others, in expressing anger anyway. For she had struck not only against the domestic "mould" she saw as maliciously constraining, but also against Walter, who she thought put her there, flaunted his undeserved superiority and power, and then mocked and cursed her efforts to break free. Sometimes she still busied herself staying "content" within the mould—for she "loved him well." More often she exploded—either against Walter, or, in more rational moments, against male-female social expectations she knew were not Walter's fault. As her poem, "The Answer," written that same fall makes clear, she saw herself in a life and death struggle.

> A maid was asked in marriage. Wise as fair,
> She gave her answer with deep thought and prayer.
>
> Expecting in the holy name of wife
> Great work, great pain, and greater joy in life.
>
> Such work she found as brainless slaves might do;
> By day and night, long labor, never through.

Such pain—no language can such pain reveal;
It had no limit but her power to feel.

Such joy life left in her sad soul's employ
Neither the hope nor memory of joy.

Helpless she died, with one despairing cry
"I thought it good! How could I tell the lie!"

And answered Nature, merciful and stern,
"I teach by killing. Let the others learn."

Charlotte knew perfectly well that many of her experiences, as well as her ideas, paralleled those of other women. It was probably that kind of confidence (as well as unhappiness) that inspired her to send "The Answer" to the *Woman's Journal,* official organ of the American Woman Suffrage Association. She already had contacts with the Boston-based suffrage organization through her Beecher relatives. Perhaps it was partly because of family connections that they published it. But Alice Stone Blackwell, then an editor for the *Journal,* must have also liked her work, because she gave Charlotte immense encouragement: first prize for "The Answer," a year's free subscription, and also a regular flow of congratulatory letters as Charlotte sent her other articles and poems. Alice Stone Blackwell, daughter of the famed Lucy Stone and Henry Blackwell team, and niece of the pioneering women doctors Elizabeth and Emily Blackwell, had been collecting, editing, and writing many of the crisp hard-headed articles that had spearheaded the women's movement for several years. Since Charlotte had been studying them carefully, and was now writing her own, it was not a question of whether but of when she would begin to participate more directly in women's political affairs, meet more of the leaders, and attend their annual conventions.

Her first suffrage convention was this same fall, 1886, Lucy Stone and Henry Blackwell presiding. In her diary, Charlotte described Lucy Stone in modest terms: she was a "lovely motherly sweet little woman with a soft quiet voice." Apparently, seventy-one-year-old Lucy Stone's appearance came as something of a surprise, for there was nothing "sweet" and "soft" about her reputation. Hard-working, forceful, a reformer to the core, Lucy Stone had been an abolitionist, a temperance worker, a captivating leader of the women's movement for over twenty years. Along with Henry Blackwell, Julia Ward Howe, and others, Lucy Stone had helped found the American Woman Suffrage Association and, even more importantly perhaps, had helped found, edit, and largely finance the weekly *Woman's Journal,* which Charlotte turned to constantly for pointers and cues.

Meanwhile, by the early winter of 1886, Charlotte was waging a two-front public–private battle, her published articles and verse reflecting her efforts to use analytic tools, her diaries reflecting her more fitful outbursts. For instance, in an article, "Why Women Do Not Reform Their Dress?" she analyzed some of the sources of her anger. It was plain to her that dress reformers had to face "friends' constant disapprobation, ridicule, [and] opposition," and that their nonconformity in dress caused "an uneasy sense of isolation and disagreeable noticeability, loss of social position, constant mortification and shame." She concluded that women had to combat their "miseducated sense of beauty and fitness." Those were feelings Charlotte explained theoretically, but also felt keenly, as her diaries make clear. For instance, she got furious with her cousin Robert Brown: he "makes an ass of himself by his loudmouthed contempt of women's rights and other justice. It is hard to be despised by such men as that." And since she apparently could not fight Walter on the women's issue directly (he was far more supportive than most males in the 1880s would have been), she attacked him in other ways instead, like sauntering over to his studio and carping at his art work. In fact, one time she criticized his painting "so harshly from a moral point of view that he smashes it and burns it." Tears followed, as did profuse apologies, as did carping sprees again.

In fact, tensions seemed to increase all the time. The more Charlotte worked at painting, writing, or even housework, the worse the fights. Her painting created competition; her writing meant that private problems were publicly exposed (indirectly, but accurately enough to antagonize Walter); and housework fed resentments which brought on exasperating scenes. With all this going on, Charlotte's diary entry at the end of the year was remarkably optimistic.

> I leave behind me tonight a year of much happiness, growth, and progress; also of great misery. But the happiness and progress are real and well founded; and the misery was owing mainly to a diseased condition of the nervous system. It is past, I hope forever.
>
> I have become a person more in harmony with my surroundings; better fitted to live peacefully among my friends; and yet have not lost a keen interest in the world's work. I can write and paint better than before; and think as well when I am strong enough.
>
> But I certainly have lost much of my self-abandoning enthusiasm and fierce determination in the cause of right. Perhaps it is as well for the ultimate work done. I do not feel so. I feel in some ways lowered—degraded—traitor to my cause. But I am not sure, it may be a lingering trace of the disordered

period just passed. When I know myself to be *well* in all ways I can better judge.

I have written half a play this year and a little good poetry. Also some painting and drawing which has been very profitable to me as work. This is an immense gain on last year and that before. At any rate, I feel happy and contented with my home and family; and have hope and courage for the New Year.

May it be fruitful and good!

Early in the year, in February 1887, Charlotte found a new opportunity to test her commitment to the "cause of right." Having established some reputation for herself as a contributor to the *Woman's Journal,* she was asked by Alice Stone Blackwell to manage a suffrage column for a Providence labor-oriented weekly newspaper called the *People.* On February 20, 1887, she noted that she had had a "good talk" with a certain Mrs. Smythe, who was "another victim" with a "sickly child" and an ignorant husband who was "using his 'marital rights' at her vital expense." That same day, she decided to accept Miss Blackwell's offer.

Charlotte's feminist writings were taking her in new directions, to contacts, albeit indirect ones, with political activists rather different in style and purpose from the reform-oriented thinkers she had been accustomed to. Reform Darwinists, Social Gospel leaders, academic and religious proponents of progress in the name of justice and right—these Charlotte had studied and admired. Most of her friends and cousins had reform inclinations, or reform-minded fathers anyway—William Channing, Rowland Hazard, Edward Everett Hale. Most of her author-heroes proclaimed the necessity for progressive social change. They used "law of nature" arguments, usually "scientific" evolutionary ones, to defend their view that man had an ethical, moral, and religious responsibility to use intelligence and reason to improve society in accordance with God's design.

But Charlotte must have noticed right away that articles in the *People* had a different and more radical cast. In the first issue of the paper (1885), the editors had openly declared their intention to "advocate co-operation and the rightfulness, the duty, and the benefits of labor partnerships, or trade unionism as it is sometimes called," and to publicize "the difficulties, dangers and privations with which all classes of workers have to contend." The founding of the *People* reflected a national trend: a rapidly expanding protest spirit, rising tension, strikes, violence. Openly committed to providing a pro-labor analysis of contemporary politics, the *People* was sponsored by a Rhode Island chapter of the Knights of Labor, a national organization founded in 1869 by Uriah Stephens, and boasting, by 1887, more than a half a million members across the country. According to some, the mounting labor pressure resulted partly from the Haymarket tragedy of 1886. For more than any other single event of the decade, it dramatized, in brutal form, what the conflict between capital and labor really meant.

The Haymarket incident was the culmination of a series of labor disputes at the McCormick Harvester factory in Chicago, Illinois, in the winter and spring of 1886. A lockout of some 1,400 impoverished workers in February was followed by a strike, by intermittent violence, and finally by a mass protest meeting called for the evening of May 4. A bomb exploded, the police opened fire, several people were killed, and over one hundred were severely wounded. Eight political activists were convicted of conspiracy to murder; their inflammatory speeches were said to have caused the violence. The press vilified their anarchist connections and called for retribution; three of them were later hanged. It was the cause célèbre of American radicals of the 1880s, sensitizing many to the grotesque inequities in society, but also intensifying popular suspicion of those who challenged the majority's complacency.

Very few contemporaries of Charlotte's class and background were enthusiastic supporters of the Chicago labor leaders. One of her heroes, political cartoonist Thomas Nast, condemned them. Even many labor leaders chose to look the other way. Still, the incident was symptomatic, and the restive labor spirit too contagious to be easily subdued. High rates of unemployment, the grim monotony of the factory scene, the below subsistence wages, child labor, unsafe working conditions—all these were attracting the attention not only of male intellectual and organizational reformers but also of the women's rights proponents whom Charlotte was coming to admire.

Like many of her contemporaries, however, and like many feminists before her, Charlotte would take a rather circuitous route toward identification with the labor cause; and in 1887 she had just begun. Only vaguely did she understand working-class grievances and programs; and only rarely had she learned about their life-conditions either from experience or from books. Upper middle class in a good deal of her outlook and training, she had developed her political perspectives not from the Henry George, *Progress and Poverty,* kind of reading, certainly not from activist pro-labor tracts, but from the more rarefied Darwinist and Reform Darwinist debates instead. In fact, she had become something of a Reform Darwinist herself. She was impressed by evolutionary analyses of the causes of human inequality, needless suffering, pervasive social ills, and she had her "fierce dedication to the cause of right." But in part because she had experienced too little beyond books and family life, she could (as yet) only vaguely relate her ideals and theories to the practical realities of modern industrial life.

When Charlotte was asked to write a suffrage column for the *People*, it seems likely that she had no clearly formulated views of the Knights of Labor, or even of the labor movement generally, but that she had strong pro-labor sympathies nonetheless, and ones which her identification with the women's movement were strengthening all the time. Still, for the moment, it was women's issues—middle-class ones at that—which she knew and thought most about, and which her *People* articles reflect.

On March 5, 1887, the editors of the *People* introduced Charlotte's suffrage column by saying, "since the vast majority of women are workers, it must concern chiefly the working women." Probably they meant women working for miniscule pay and long hours, women of the labor movement, women organizing to better their wages and working conditions. Charlotte spoke of other kinds of working women instead: career women whose public achievements were unrecognized, or housewives who were confined to unskilled, involuntary, unpaid domestic work at home. For instance, in her first column, she bemoaned the neglect of women's inventions: By 1886, women had received 1,935 patents, but some people said they never invented anything. (She borrowed the idea from the soon-to-be-prominent muckraker Ida Tarbell.) Her second article pointed out that "woman can take an interest in the world's work and housework too; can take her place as citizen and not lose her place as wife and mother." By March she had warmed up to the issue which most bothered her: "Men have for so long exercised political power in the world that they have come to look upon it as a masculine attribute, like the beard. . . . Then they have the habit of all the ages to make them feel superior to women; so it will naturally take some time for them to recognize our equality." Women are not emotionally inferior, she continued. "Men call us emotional because they know us mostly in emotional relations, they meet only that side of our natures."

Occasionally, the suffrage column discussed other political and economic issues, and sometimes rather forcefully so. For instance, in August there was an article on the unjust inequalities of women's wages: "In Massachusetts there are more than two hundred thousand women who earn their support, by working outside of their own homes, at less than ½ the wages paid men." There were reports on working women's demands for equal pay for equal work, for "equal opportunity to learn and practice diversified industries," for equal power in the labor movement. And by September, the writing sounded like that of a labor-oriented suffrage pro: "Twenty thousand women Knights of Labor are organized, in the city of New York alone, for mutual protection. Like the fabled Amazons, they are ready to assert and defend their rights, but not, as they did, with the sword. Organized labor demands the ballot for them."

Those were strong-sounding statements, increasingly radical ones at that, if only we could be certain whether Charlotte wrote them, or whether the *People* reprinted articles from other journals when Charlotte did not have time or energy to write.* Nevertheless, a number of articles probably reflect political perspectives Charlotte was beginning to develop, but not, as yet, ones that she could call her own.

Most of the articles Charlotte wrote for the *People* focused on an issue that, at this juncture, seemed paramount to her: the conflict between marriage and career. Marriage, she told her readers, "is what you are born for, trained for, taught for; it is at once your destiny and desire, your hope and your necessity." But she felt that women needed work as well as love: "Let girls learn a trade or profession as well as boys, and have an individual independent life of their own; then they will not have to spin webs for a living." Charlotte did not claim that her ideas were original. On the contrary, she was busy finding pithy passages of celebrities to quote, passages of her aunt Harriet Beecher Stowe, for instance, who was ending her career just as Charlotte was fitfully beginning hers. Charlotte quoted her aunt: "Every woman has rights as a human being first, which belong to no sex, and ought to be as freely conceded to her as if she were a man—and first and foremost, the great right of doing anything which God and nature evidently have fitted her to excel in."

That was Charlotte's view exactly: Women, "first and foremost," must secure their rights as people, be independent, develop their own integrity. If they do not, if they marry first, their nuptial vows are simply meaningless. It was almost as though Charlotte were using the *People* column to test—theoretically and publicly—her own private emotional dilemma: in "the marriage ceremony the bride is made to promise to 'love and honor.' But she sometimes finds that neither love nor honor is possible."

---

* A number of these articles for the *People* suffrage column were unsigned.

PAULA A. TREICHLER

Escaping the Sentence:
Diagnosis and Discourse in
"The Yellow Wallpaper"
(1987)

Almost immediately in Charlotte Perkins Gilman's story "The Yellow Wallpaper," the female narrator tells us she is "sick." Her husband, "a physician of high standing," has diagnosed her as having a "temporary nervous depression—a slight hysterical tendency."[1] Yet her journal—in whose words the story unfolds—records her own resistance to this diagnosis and, tentatively, her suspicion that the medical treatment it dictates—treatment that confines her to a room in an isolated country estate—will not cure her. She suggests that the diagnosis itself, by undermining her own conviction that her "condition" is serious and real, may indeed be one reason why she does not get well.

A medical diagnosis is a verbal formula representing a constellation of physical symptoms and observable behaviors. Once formulated, it dictates a series of therapeutic actions: In "The Yellow Wallpaper," the diagnosis of hysteria or depression, conventional "women's diseases" of the nineteenth century, sets in motion a therapeutic regimen which involves language in several ways. The narrator is forbidden to engage in normal social conversation; her physical isolation is in part designed to remove her from the possibility of over-stimulating intellectual discussion. She is further encouraged to exercise "self-control" and avoid expressing negative thoughts and fears about her illness; she is also urged to keep her fancies and superstitions in check. Above all, she is forbidden to "work"—to write. Learning to monitor her own speech, she develops an artificial feminine self who reinforces the terms of her husband's expert diagnosis: this self attempts to speak reasonably and in "a very quiet voice," refrains from crying in his presence, and hides the fact that she is keeping a journal. This male-identified self disguises the true underground narrative: a confrontation with language.

---

[1] Charlotte Perkins Gilman, *The Yellow Wallpaper* (Old Westbury, N.Y.: The Feminist Press, 1973), p. 13. Subsequent references are cited parenthetically in the text.

Because she does not feel free to speak truthfully "to a living soul," she confides her thoughts to a journal—"dead paper"—instead. The only safe language is dead language. But even the journal is not altogether safe. The opening passages are fragmented as the narrator retreats from topic after topic (the first journal entry consists of 39 separate paragraphs). The three points at which her language becomes more discursive carry more weight by contrast. These passages seem at first to involve seemingly unobjectionable, safe topics: the house, her room, and the room's yellow wallpaper. Indeed, the very first mention of the wallpaper expresses conventional hyperbole: "I never saw worse paper in my life." But the language at once grows unexpected and intense:

> One of those sprawling flamboyant patterns committing every artistic sin. It is dull enough to confuse the eye in following, pronounced enough to constantly irritate and provoke study, and when you follow the lame uncertain curves for a little distance they suddenly commit suicide—plunge off at outrageous angles, destroy themselves in unheard of contradictions. (13)

Disguised as an acceptable feminine topic (interest in decor), the yellow wallpaper comes to occupy the narrator's entire reality. Finally, she rips it from the walls to reveal its real meaning. Unveiled, the yellow wallpaper is a metaphor for women's discourse. From a conventional perspective, it first seems strange, flamboyant, confusing, outrageous: the very act of women's writing produces discourse which embodies "unheard of contradictions." Once freed, it expresses what is elsewhere kept hidden and embodies patterns that the patriarchal order ignores, suppresses, fears as grotesque, or fails to perceive at all. Like all good metaphors, the yellow wallpaper is variously interpreted by readers to represent (among other things) the "pattern" which underlies sexual inequality, the external manifestation of neurasthenia, the narrator's unconscious, the narrator's situation within patriarchy.[2] But an

---

[2] Umberto Eco describes a "good metaphor" as one which, like a good joke, offers a shortcut through the labyrinth of limitless semiosis. "Metaphor, Dictionary, and Encyclopedia," *New Literary History*, 15 (Winter 1984), 255–71. Though there is relatively little criticism on "The Yellow Wallpaper" to date, the wallpaper seems to be a fruitful metaphor for discussions of madness, women's relationship to medicine, sexual inequality, marriage, economic dependence, and sexuality. An introduction to these issues is provided by Elaine R. Hedges in her "Afterword," *The Yellow Wallpaper*, pp. 37–63. Hedges also cites a number of nineteenth-century responses to the story. A useful though condescending discussion of the story in the light of Gilman's own life is Mary A. Hill, "Charlotte Perkins Gilman: A Feminist's Struggle with Womanhood," *Massachusetts Review*, 21 (Fall 1980), 503–26. A

emphasis on discourse—writing, the act of speaking, language—draws us to the central issue in this particular story: the narrator's alienation from work, writing, and intellectual life. Thus the story is inevitably concerned with the complicated and charged relationship between women and language: analysis then illuminates particular points of conflict between patriarchal language and women's discourse. This conflict in turn raises a number of questions relevant for both literary and feminist scholarship: In what senses can language be said to be oppressive to women? How do feminist linguistic innovations seek to escape this oppression? What is the relationship of innovation to material conditions? And what does it mean, theoretically, to escape the sentence that the structure of patriarchal language imposes?

I. THE YELLOW WALLPAPER

The narrator of "The Yellow Wallpaper" has come with her husband to an isolated country estate for the summer. The house, a "colonial mansion," has been untenanted for years through some problem with inheritance. It is "the most beautiful place!" The grounds contain "hedges and walls and gates that lock, and lots of separate little houses for the gardeners and people" (11). Despite this palatial potential to accommodate many people, the estate is virtually deserted with nothing growing in its greenhouses. The narrator perceives "something queer about it" and believes it may be haunted.

She is discouraged in this and other fancies by her sensible physician—husband who credits only what is observable, scientific, or demonstrable through facts and figures. He has scientifically diagnosed his wife's condition as merely "a temporary nervous depression"; her brother, also a noted physician, concurs in this opinion. Hence husband and wife have come as physician and patient to this solitary summer mansion in quest of cure. The narrator reports her medical regimen to her journal, together with her own view of the problem:

> So I take phosphates or phosphites—whichever it is, and tonics, and journeys, and air, and exercise, and am absolutely forbidden to "work" until I am well again.

Bachelardian critical reading is Mary Beth Pringle, "'La Poétique de l'Espace' in Charlotte Perkins Gilman's 'The Yellow Wallpaper,'" *The French-American Review*, 3 (Winter 1978/ Spring 1979), 15–22. See also Loralee MacPike, "Environment as Psychopathological Symbolism in 'The Yellow Wallpaper,'" *American Literary Realism 1870–1910*, 8 (Summer 1975), 286–88, and Beate Schopp-Schilling, "'The Yellow Wallpaper': A Rediscovered 'Realistic' Story," *American Literary Realism 1870–1910*, 8 (Summer 1975), 284–86.

Personally, I disagree with their ideas.
Personally, I believe that congenial work, with excitement and change, would
do me good.
But what is one to do? (10)

Her room at the top of the house seems once to have been a nursery or
a playroom with bars on the windows and "rings and things on the walls."
The room contains not much more than a mammoth metal bed. The ugly
yellow wallpaper has been stripped off in patches—perhaps by the children
who formerly inhabited the room. In this "atrocious nursery" the narrator
increasingly spends her time. Her husband is often away on medical cases,
her baby makes her nervous, and no other company is permitted her. Disturbed by the wallpaper, she asks for another room or for different paper; her
husband urges her not to give way to her "fancies." Further, he claims that
any change would lead to more change: "after the wallpaper was changed it
would be the heavy bedstead, and then the barred windows, and then that
gate at the head of the stairs, and so on" (14). So no changes are made, and
the narrator is left alone with her "imaginative power and habit of story-
making" (15). In this stimulus-deprived environment, the "pattern" of the
wallpaper becomes increasingly compelling: the narrator gradually becomes
intimate with its "principle of design" and unconventional connections. The
figure of a woman begins to take shape behind the superficial pattern of the
paper. The more the wallpaper comes alive, the less inclined is the narrator
to write in her journal—"dead paper." Now with three weeks left of the
summer and her relationship with the wallpaper more and more intense, she
asks once more to be allowed to leave. Her husband refuses: "I cannot possibly leave town just now. Of course if you were in any danger, I could and
would, but you really are better, dear, whether you can see it or not. I am a
doctor, dear, and I know" (23). She expresses the fear that she is not getting
well. "Bless her little heart!" he responds, "She shall be as sick as she pleases"
(24). When she hesitantly voices the belief that she may be losing her mind,
he reproaches her so vehemently that she says no more. Instead, in the final
weeks of the summer, she gives herself up to the wallpaper. "Life is very
much more exciting now than it used to be," she tells her journal. "You see I
have something more to expect, to look forward to, to watch. I really do eat
better, and am more quiet than I was" (27). She reports that her husband
judges her "to be flourishing in spite of my wallpaper."

She begins to strip off the wallpaper at every opportunity in order to free
the woman she perceives is trapped inside. She becomes increasingly aware
of this woman and other female figures creeping behind the surface pattern
of the wallpaper: there is a hint that the room's previous female occupant has

left behind the marks of her struggle for freedom. Paranoid by now, the narrator attempts to disguise her obsession with the wallpaper. On the last day, she locks herself in the room and succeeds in stripping off most of the remaining paper. When her husband comes home and finally unlocks the door, he is horrified to find her creeping along the walls of the room. "I've got out at last," she tells him triumphantly, "And I've pulled off most of the paper, so you can't put me back" (36). Her husband faints, and she is obliged to step over him each time she circles the room.

"The Yellow Wallpaper" was read by nineteenth-century readers as a harrowing case study of neurasthenia. Even recent readings have treated the narrator's madness as a function of her individual psychological situation. A feminist reading emphasizes the social and economic conditions which drive the narrator—and potentially all women—to madness. In these readings, the yellow wallpaper represents (1) the narrator's own mind, (2) the narrator's unconscious, (3) the "pattern" of social and economic dependence which reduces women to domestic slavery. The woman in the wallpaper represents (1) the narrator herself, gone mad, (2) the narrator's unconscious, (3) all women. While these interpretations are plausible and fruitful, I interpret the wallpaper to be women's writing or women's discourse, and the woman in the wallpaper to be the representation of women that becomes possible only after women obtain the right to speak. In this reading, the yellow wallpaper stands for a new vision of women—one which is constructed differently from the representation of women in patriarchal language. The story is thus in part about the clash between two modes of discourse: one powerful, "ancestral," and dominant; the other new, "impertinent," and visionary. The story's outcome makes a statement about the relationship of a visionary feminist project to material reality.

II. DIAGNOSIS AND DISCOURSE

It is significant that the narrator of "The Yellow Wallpaper" is keeping a journal, confiding to "dead paper" the unorthodox thoughts and perceptions she is reluctant to tell to a "living soul." Challenging and subverting the expert prescription that forbids her to write, the journal evokes a sense of urgency and danger. "There comes John," she tells us at the end of her first entry, "and I must put this away,—he hates to have me write a word" (13). We, her readers, are thus from the beginning her confidantes, implicated in forbidden discourse.

Contributing to our suspense and sense of urgency is the ambiguity of the narrator's "condition," whose etiology is left unstated in the story. For her physician–husband, it is a medical condition of unknown origin to be medically managed. Certain imagery (the "ghostliness" of the estate, the "trouble" with the heirs) suggests hereditary disease. Other evidence points toward psychological causes (e.g., postpartum depression, failure to adjust to marriage and motherhood). A feminist analysis moves beyond such localized causes to implicate the economic and social conditions which, under patriarchy, make women domestic slaves. In any case, the fact that the origin of the narrator's condition is never made explicit intensifies the role of diagnosis in putting a name to her "condition."

Symptoms are crucial for the diagnostic process. The narrator reports, among other things, exhaustion, crying, nervousness, synesthesia, anger, paranoia, and hallucination. "Temporary nervous depression" (coupled with a "slight hysterical tendency") is the medical term that serves to diagnose or define these symptoms. Once pronounced, and reinforced by the second opinion of the narrator's brother, this diagnosis not only names reality but also has considerable power over what that reality is now to be: it dictates the narrator's removal to the "ancestral halls" where the story is set and generates a medical therapeutic regimen that includes physical isolation, "phosphates and phosphites," air, and rest. Above all, it forbids her to "work." The quotation marks, registering her husband's perspective, discredit the equation of writing with true work. The diagnostic language of the physician is coupled with the paternalistic language of the husband to create a formidable array of controls over her behavior.

I use "diagnosis," then, as a metaphor for the voice of medicine or science that speaks to define women's condition. Diagnosis is powerful and public; representing institutional authority, it dictates that money, resources, and space are to be expended as consequences in the "real world." It is a male voice that privileges the rational, the practical, and the observable. It is the voice of male logic and male judgment which dismisses superstition and refuses to see the house as haunted or the narrator's condition as serious. It imposes controls on the female narrator and dictates how she is to perceive and talk about the world. It is enforced by the "ancestral halls" themselves: the rules are followed even when the physician–husband is absent. In fact, the opening imagery—"ancestral halls," "a colonial mansion," "a haunted house"—legitimizes the diagnostic process by placing it firmly within an institutional frame: medicine, marriage, patriarchy. All function in the story to define and prescribe.

In contrast, the narrator in her nursery room speaks privately to her journal. At first she expresses her views hesitantly, "personally." Her language includes a number of stereotypical features of "women's language": not only are its topics limited, it is marked formally by exclamation marks, italics, intensifiers, and repetition of the impotent refrain, "What is one to do?"[3] The journal entries at this early stage are very tentative and clearly shaped under the stern eye of male judgment. Oblique references only hint at an alternative reality. The narrator writes, for example, that the wallpaper has been "torn off" and "stripped away," yet she does not say by whom. Her qualms about her medical diagnosis and treatment remain unspoken except in her journal, which functions only as a private respite, a temporary relief. "Dead paper," it is not truly subversive.

Nevertheless, the narrator's language almost from the first does serve to call into question both the diagnosis of her condition and the rules established to treat it. As readers, therefore, we are not permitted wholehearted confidence in the medical assessment of the problem. It is not that we doubt the existence of her "condition," for it obviously causes genuine suffering; but we come to doubt that the diagnosis names the real problem—the narrator seems to place her own inverted commas around the words "temporary nervous depression" and "slight hysterical tendency"—and perceive that whatever its nature it is exacerbated by the rules established for its cure.

For this reason, we are alert to the possibility of an alternative vision. The yellow wallpaper provides it. Representing a different reality, it is "living paper," aggressively alive: "You think you have mastered it, but just as you get well underway in following, it turns a back-somersault and there you are. It slaps you in the face, knocks you down, and tramples upon you. It is like a bad dream" (25). The narrator's husband refuses to replace the wallpaper, "whitewash" the room, or let her change rooms altogether on the grounds that other changes will then be demanded. The wallpaper is to remain: acknowledgment of its reality is the first step toward freedom. Confronting it at first through male eyes, the narrator is repelled and speculates that the children who inhabited the room before her attacked it for its ugliness. There is thus considerable resistance to the wallpaper and an implied rejection of what it represents, even by young children.

---

[3] "Women's language" is discussed in Robin Lakoff, *Language and Woman's Place* (New York: Harper and Row, 1975); Casey Miller and Kate Swift, *Words and Women* (New York: Anchor/Doubleday, 1976); Barrie Thorne, Cheris Kramarae, and Nancy Henley, eds., "Introduction," *Language, Gender and Society* (Rowley, Mass.: Newbury House, 1983); Cheris Kramarae, *Women and Men Speaking* (Rowley, Mass.: Newbury House, 1981); Sally McConnell-Ginet, Ruth Borker, and Nelly Furman, eds., *Women and Language in Literature and Society* (New York: Praeger, 1980); Mary Ritchie Key, *Male/Female Language* (Metuchen, New Jersey: Scarecrow Press, 1975); and Paula A. Treichler, "Verbal Subversions in Dorothy Parker: 'Trapped like a Trap in a Trap,'" *Language and Style,* 13 (Fall 1980), 46–61.

But the wallpaper exerts its power and, at the same time, the narrator's journal entries falter; "I don't know why I should write this" (21), she says, about halfway through the story. She makes a final effort to be allowed to leave the room; when this fails, she becomes increasingly absorbed by the wallpaper and by the figure of a woman that exists behind its confusing surface pattern. This figure grows clearer to her, to the point where she can join her behind the paper and literally act within it. At this point, her language becomes bolder: she completes the predicates that were earlier left passively hanging. Describing joint action with the woman in the wallpaper, she tells us that the room has come to be damaged at the hands of women: "I pulled and she shook, I shook and she pulled, and before morning we had peeled off yards of that paper" (32); "I am getting angry enough to do something desperate" (34). From an increasingly distinctive perspective, she sees an alternative reality beneath the repellent surface pattern in which the figures of women are emerging. Her original perception is confirmed: the patriarchal house is indeed "haunted" by figures of women. The room is revealed as a prison inhabited by its former inmates, whose struggles have nearly destroyed it. Absorbed almost physically by "living paper"—writing—she strives to liberate the women trapped within the ancestral halls, women with whom she increasingly identifies. Once begun, liberation and identification are irreversible: "I've got out at last . . ." cries the narrator, "And I've pulled off most of the paper, so you can't put me back!" (36).

This ending of "The Yellow Wallpaper" is ambiguous and complex. Because the narrator's final proclamation is both triumphant and horrifying, madness in the story is both positive and negative. On the one hand, it testifies to an alternative reality and challenges patriarchy head on. The fact that her unflappable husband faints when he finds her establishes the dramatic power of her new freedom. Defying the judgment that she suffers from a "temporary nervous depression," she has followed her own logic, her own perceptions, her own projects to this final scene in which madness is seen as a kind of transcendent sanity. This engagement with the yellow wallpaper constitutes a form of the "work" which has been forbidden—women's writing. As she steps over the patriarchal body, she leaves the authoritative voice of diagnosis in shambles at her feet. Forsaking "women's language" forever, her new mode of speaking—an unlawful language—escapes "the sentence" imposed by patriarchy.

On the other hand, there are consequences to be paid for this escape. As the ending of the narrative, her madness will no doubt commit her to more intense medical treatment, perhaps to the dreaded Weir Mitchell of

whom her husband has spoken. The surrender of patriarchy is only temporary: her husband has merely fainted, after all, not died, and will no doubt
move swiftly and severely to deal with her. Her individual escape is temporary and compromised.

But there is yet another sense in which "The Yellow Wallpaper" enacts
a clash between diagnosis and women's discourse. Asked once whether the
story was based on fact, Gilman replied "I had been as far as one could go
and get back."[4] Gilman based the story on her own experience of depression
and treatment. For her first visit to the noted neurologist S. Weir Mitchell,
she prepared a detailed case history of her own illness, constructed in part
from her journal entries. Mitchell was not impressed: he "only thought it
proved conceit" (*The Living*, 95). He wanted obedience from patients, not
information. "Wise women," he wrote elsewhere "choose their doctors and
trust them. The wisest ask the fewest questions."[5] Gilman reproduced in her
journal Mitchell's prescription for her:

> Live as domestic a life as possible. Have your child with you all the time.
> (Be it remarked that if I did but dress the baby it left me shaking and
> crying—certainly far from a healthy companionship for her, to say nothing
> of the effect on me.) Lie down an hour after every meal. Have but two hours
> intellectual life a day. And never touch pen, brush or pencil as long as you
> live. (*The Living*, 96)

Gilman spent several months trying to follow Mitchell's prescription, a
period of intense suffering for her:

> I could not read nor write nor paint nor sew nor talk nor listen to talking,
> nor anything. I lay on that lounge and wept all day. The tears ran down into
> my ears on either side. I went to bed crying, woke in the night crying, sat on
> the edge of the bed in the morning and cried—from sheer continuous pain.
> (*The Living*, 121)

At last in a "moment of clear vision," Gilman realized that for her the
traditional domestic role was at least in part the cause of her distress. She left

---

[4] Charlotte Perkins Gilman, *The Living of Charlotte Perkins Gilman: An Autobiography* (New York: Appleton-Century, 1935), p. 121. Subsequent references are cited parenthetically in the text.

[5] S. Weir Mitchell, *Doctor and Patient* (Philadelphia: Lippincott, 1888), p. 48.

her husband and with her baby went to California to be a writer and a feminist activist. Three years later she wrote "The Yellow Wallpaper." After the story was published, she sent a copy to Mitchell. If it in any way influenced his treatment of women in the future, she wrote, "I have not lived in vain" (*The Living*, 121).

There are several points to note here with respect to women's discourse. Gilman's use of her own journal to create a fictional journal which in turn becomes a published short story problematizes and calls our attention to the journal form. The terms "depression" and "hysteria" signal a non-textual as well as a textual conundrum: contemporary readers could (and some did) read the story as a realistic account of madness; for feminist readers (then and now) who bring to the text some comprehension of medical attitudes toward women in the nineteenth century, such a non-ironic reading is not possible. Lest we miss Gilman's point, her use of a real proper name in her story, Weir Mitchell's, draws explicit attention to the world outside the text.[6]

Thus "The Yellow Wallpaper" is not merely a fictional challenge to the patriarchal diagnosis of women's condition. It is also a public critique of a real medical treatment. Publication of the story added power and status to Gilman's words and transformed the journal form from a private to a public setting. Her published challenge to diagnosis has now been read by thousands of readers. By living to tell the tale, the woman who writes escapes the sentence that condemns her to silence.

---

[6] A feminist understanding of medical treatment of women in the nineteenth century is, however, by no means uncomplicated. An analysis frequently quoted is that by Barbara Ehrenreich and Deirdre English, *For Her Own Good: 150 Years of the Experts' Advice to Women* (Garden City, N.Y.: Anchor/Doubleday, 1979). Their analysis is critiqued by Regina Morantz, "The Lady and Her Physician," in *Clio's Consciousness Raised: New Perspectives on the History of Women,* eds. Mary S. Hartman and Lois Banner (New York: Harper Colophon, 1974), pp. 38–53; as well as by Ludi Jordanova, "Conceptualizing Power Over Women," *Radical Science Journal,* 12 (1982), 124–28. Attention to the progressive aspects of Weir Mitchell's treatment of women is given by Morantz and by Suzanne Poirier, "The Weir Mitchell Rest Cure: Four Women Who 'Took Charge,'" paper presented at the conference Women's Health: Taking Care and Taking Charge, Morgantown, West Virginia, 1982 [Author's affiliation: Humanistic Studies Program, Health Sciences Center, University of Illinois at Chicago]. See also Barbara Sicherman, "The Uses of Diagnosis: Doctors, Patients, and Neurasthenia," *Journal of the History of Medicine and Allied Sciences,* 32 (January 1977), 33–54; Carroll Smith-Rosenberg and Charles Rosenberg, "The Female Animal: Medical and Biological Views of Woman and Her Role in Nineteenth-Century America," rpt. in *Concepts of Health and Disease; Interdisciplinary Perspectives,* eds. Arthur Caplan, H. Tristram Engelhardt, Jr. and James J. McCartney (Reading, Mass.: Addison-Wesley, 1981), pp. 281–303; and Ann Douglas Wood, "'The Fashionable Diseases': Women's Complaints and

III. Escaping the Sentence

To call "The Yellow Wallpaper" a struggle between diagnosis and discourse is to characterize the story in terms of language. More precisely, it is to contrast the signification procedures of patriarchal medicine with discursive disruptions that call those procedures into question. A major problem in "The Yellow Wallpaper" involves the relationship of the linguistic sign to the signified, of language to "reality." Diagnosis, highlighted from the beginning by the implicit inverted commas and diagnostic phrases ("a slight hysterical tendency"), stands in the middle of an equation which translates a phenomenological perception of the human body into a finite set of signs called "symptoms"—fever, exhaustion, nervousness, pallor, and so on—which are in turn assembled to produce a "diagnosis"; this sign generates treatment, a set of prescriptions that impinge once more upon the "real" human body. Part of the power of diagnosis as a scientific process depends upon a notion of language as transparent, as *not* the issue. Rather the issue is the precision, efficiency, and plausibility with which a correct diagnostic sign is generated by a particular state of affairs that is assumed to exist in reality. In turn, the diagnostic sign is not complete until its clinical implications have been elaborated as a set of concrete therapeutic practices designed not merely to refer to but actually to change the original physical reality. Chary with its diagnostic categories (as specialized lexicons go), medicine's rich and intricate descriptive vocabulary testifies to the history of its mission: to translate the realities of the human body into human language and back again. As such, it is a perfect example of language which "reflects" reality and simultaneously "produces" it.[7]

Why is this interesting? And why is this process important in "The Yellow Wallpaper"? Medical diagnosis stands as a prime example of an authorized linguistic process (distilled, respected, high-paying) whose representational claims are strongly supported by social, cultural, and economic practices. Even more than most forms of male discourse, the diagnostic

---

Their Treatment in Nineteenth-Century America," in *Clio's Consciousness Raised: New Perspectives on the History of Women*, pp. 1–22.

[7] The notion that diagnosis is socially constituted through doctor–patient interaction is discussed by Marianne A. Paget, "On the Work of Talk: Studies in Misunderstanding," in *The Social Organization of Doctor–Patient Communication*, eds. Sue Fisher and Alexandra Dundas Todd (Washington, D.C.: Center for Applied Linguistics, 1983), pp. 55–74. See also Barbara Sicherman, "The Uses of Diagnosis."

process is multiply-sanctioned.[8] "The Yellow Wallpaper" challenges both the particular "sentence" passed on the narrator and the elaborate sentencing process whose presumed representational power can sentence women to isolation, deprivation, and alienation from their own sentencing possibilities. The right to author or originate sentences is at the heart of the story and what the yellow wallpaper represents: a figure for women's discourse, it seeks to escape the sentence passed by medicine and patriarchy. Before looking more closely at what the story suggests about the nature of women's discourse, we need to place somewhat more precisely this notion of "the sentence."

Diagnosis is a "sentence" in that it is simultaneously a linguistic entity, a declaration or judgment, and a plan for action in the real world whose clinical consequences may spell dullness, drama, or doom for the diagnosed. Diagnosis may be, then, not merely a sentence but a death sentence. This doubling of the word "sentence" is not mere playfulness. "I sat down and began to speak," wrote Anna Kavan in *Asylum Piece*, describing the beginning of a woman's mental breakdown, "driving my sluggish tongue to frame words that seemed useless even before they were uttered." This physically exhausting process of producing sentences is generalized: "Sometimes I think that some secret court must have tried and condemned me, unheard, to this heavy sentence."[9] The word "sentence" is both sign and signified, word and act, declaration and discursive consequence. Its duality emphasizes the difficulty of an analysis which privileges purely semiotic relationships on the one hand or the representational nature of language on the other. In "The Yellow Wallpaper," the diagnosis of hysteria may be a sham: it may be socially constituted or merely individually expedient quite apart from even a conventional representational relationship. But it dictates a rearrangement of material reality nevertheless. The sentence may be unjust, inaccurate, or irrelevant, but the sentence is served anyway.[10]

---

8 Discussions of the multiple sanctions for medicine and science include Shelley Day, "Is Obstetric Technology Depressing?" *Radical Science Journal*, 12 (1982), 17–45; Donna J. Haraway, "In the Beginning was the Word: The Genesis of Biological Theory," *Signs*, 6 (Spring 1981), 469–81; Bruno Latour and Steve Woolgar, *Laboratory Life: Social Construction of Scientific Facts* (Beverly Hills: Sage, 1979); Evan Stark, "What is Medicine?" *Radical Science Journal*, 12 (1982), 46–89; and P. Wright and A. Treacher, eds., *The Problem of Medical Knowledge* (Edinburgh: Edinburgh University Press, 1982).

9 Anna Kavan, *Asylum Piece* (1940; rpt. New York: Michael Kesend, 1981), pp. 63, 65.

10 Reviewing medical evidence in "The Yellow Wallpaper," Suzanne Poirier suggests that a diagnosis of "neurasthenia" would have been more precise but that in any case, given the narrator's symptoms, the treatment was inappropriate and probably harmful. "'The Yellow Wallpaper' as Medical Case History," paper presented to the Faculty Seminar in Medicine

The sentence is of particular importance in modern linguistics, where it has dominated inquiry for twenty-five years and for more than seventy years has been the upper cut-off point for the study of language: consideration of word sequences and meaning beyond the sentence has been typically dismissed as too untidy and speculative for linguistic science. The word "sentence" also emphasizes the technical concentration, initiated by structuralism but powerfully developed by transformational grammar, on syntax (formal grammatical structure at the sentence level). The formulaic sentences S→NP + VP which initiates the familiar tree diagram of linguistic analysis could well be said to exemplify the tyranny of syntax over the study of semantics (meaning) and pragmatics (usage). As a result, as Sally McConnell-Ginet has argued, linguistics has often failed to address those aspects of language with which women have been most concerned: on the one hand, the semantic or non-linguistic conditions underlying given grammatical structures, and on the other, the contextual circumstances in which linguistic structures are actually used.[11] One can generalize and say that signs alone are of less interest to women than are the processes of signification which link signs to semantic and pragmatic aspects of speaking. To "escape the sentence" is to move beyond the boundaries of formal syntax.

---

and Society, University of Illinois College of Medicine at Urbana–Champaign, April 13, 1983. On the more general point, two recent contrasting analyses are offered by Umberto Eco, "Metaphor, Dictionary, Encyclopedia," who poses a world of language resonant with purely semiotic, intertextual relationships, and John Haiman, "Dictionaries and Encyclopedias," *Lingua*, 50 (1980), 329–57, who argues for the total interrelatedness of linguistic and cultural knowledge.

[11] Sally McConnell-Ginet, "Linguistics and the Feminist Challenge," in *Women and Language in Literature and Society*, pp. 3–25. The linguistic formula S→NP + VP means that Sentence is rewritten from this formula. Sentences are "generated" as tree diagrams that move downward from the abstract entity S to individual components of actual sentences. It could be said that linguistics misses the forest for the trees. But the fact that the study of women and language *has* concentrated on meaning and usage does not mean that syntax might not be relevant for feminist analysis. Potentially fruitful areas might include analysis of passive versus active voice (for example, see my "The Construction of Ambiguity in *The Awakening*: A Linguistic Analysis," in *Women and Language in Literature and Society*, pp. 239–57), of nominalization (a linguistic process particularly characteristic of male bureaucracies and technologies), of cases (showing underlying agency and other relationships), of negation and interrogation (two grammatical processes implicated by "women's language," Note 3), and of the relationship between deep and surface structure. Julia Penelope Stanley has addressed a number of these areas; see, for example, "Passive Motivation," *Foundations of Language*, 13 (1975), 25–39. Pronominalization, of course, has been a focus for feminist analysis for some time.

But is it to move beyond language? In writing about language over the last fifteen years, most feminist scholars in the United States have argued that language creates as well as reflects reality and hence that feminist linguistic innovation helps foster more enlightened social conditions for women. A more conservative position holds that language merely reflects social reality and that linguistic reform is hollow unless accompanied by changes in attitudes and socioeconomic conditions that also favor women's equality. Though different, particularly in their support for innovation, both positions more or less embody a view that there *is* a non-linguistic reality to which language is related in systematic ways.[12] Recent European writing challenges the transparency of such a division, arguing that at some level reality is inescapably linguistic. The account of female development within this framework emphasizes the point at which the female child comes into language (and becomes a being now called female); because she is female, she is from the first alienated from the processes of symbolic representation. Within this symbolic order, a phallocentric order, she is frozen, confined, curtailed, limited, and represented as "lack," as "other." To make a long story short, there is as yet no escaping the sentence of male-determining discourse.[13]

According to this account, "the sentence," for women, is inescapably bound up with the symbolic order. Within language, says Luce Irigaray for example, women's fate is a "death sentence."[14] Irigaray's linguistic innovations attempt to disrupt this "law of the father" and exemplify the

---

[12] See for example, Maija Blaubergs, "An Analysis of Classic Arguments Against Changing Sexist Language," in *The Voices and Words of Women and Men*, ed., Cheris Kramarae (Oxford: Pergamon Press, 1980), pp. 135–47; Francine Frank, "Women's Language in America: Myth and Reality," in *Women's Language and Style*, eds. Douglas Butturff and Edmund L. Epstein (Akron, Ohio: L&S Books, 1978), pp. 47–61; Mary Daly, *Gyn/Ecology* (Boston: Beacon, 1978); and Wendy Martyna, "The Psychology of the Generic Masculine," in *Women and Language in Literature and Society*, pp. 69–78. A general source is Barrie Thorne, Cheris Kramarae, and Nancy Henley, eds., *Language, Gender and Society* (Rowley, Mass.: Newbury House, 1983).

[13] See, for example, Juliet Mitchell and Jacqueline Rose, eds., *Feminine Sexuality: Jacques Lacan and the école freudienne* (New York: W. W. Norton, 1982), pp. 1–57.

[14] Luce Irigaray, "Veiled Lips," trans. Sara Speidel, *Mississippi Review*, 33 (Winter/Spring 1983), 99. See also Luce Irigaray, "Women's Exile: Interview with Luce Irigaray," trans. Couze Venn, *Ideology and Consciousness*, 1 (1977), 62–76; and Cary Nelson, "Envoys of Otherness: Difference and Continuity in Feminist Criticism," in *For Alma Mater: Theory and Practice in Feminist Scholarship*, eds. Paula A. Treichler, Cheris Kramarae, and Beth Stafford (Urbana: University of Illinois Press, 1985), pp. 91–118.

possibilities for a female language which "has nothing to do with the syntax which we have used for centuries, namely, that constructed according to the following organization: subject, predicate, or, subject, verb, object."[15] Whatever the realities of that particular claim, at the moment there are persuasive theoretical, professional, and political reasons for feminists to pay attention to what I will now more officially call discourse, which encompasses linguistic and formalistic considerations, yet goes beyond strict formalism to include both semantics and pragmatics. It is thus concerned not merely with speech, but with the conditions of speaking. With this notion of "sentencing," I have tried to suggest a process of language production in which an individual word, speech, or text is linked to the conditions under which it was (and could have been) produced as well as to those under which it is (and could be) read and interpreted. Thus the examination of diagnosis and discourse in a text is at once a study of a set of representational practices, of mechanisms for control and opportunities for resistance, and of communicational possibilities in fiction and elsewhere.[16]

In "The Yellow Wallpaper" we see consequences of the "death sentence." Woman is represented as childlike and dysfunctional. Her complaints are wholly circular, merely confirming the already-spoken patriarchal diagnosis. She is constituted and defined within the patriarchal order of language and destined, like Athena in Irigaray's analysis, to repeat her father's discourse "without much understanding."[17] "Personally," she says, and "I sometimes fancy": this is acceptable language in the ancestral halls. Her attempts to engage in different, serious language—self-authored—are given up; to write in the absence of patriarchal sanction requires "having to be so sly about it, or else meet with heavy opposition" (10) and is too exhausting.

---

[15] Luce Irigaray, "Women's Exile," 64.

[16] See the discussion of discourse in Meaghan Morris, "A-Mazing Grace: Notes on Mary Daly's Poetics," *Intervention*, 16 (1982), 70–92.

[17] Luce Irigaray, "Veiled Lips," 99–101. According to Irigaray's account, Apollo, "the always-already-speaking," drives away the chorus of women (the Furies) who want revenge for Clytemnestra's murder. His words convey his repulsion for the chaotic, non-hierarchical female voice: "Heave in torment, black froth erupting from your lungs"; "Never touch my halls, you have no right"; "Out you flock without a herdsman—out!" Calling for the forgetting of bloodshed, Athena, embodying the father's voice and the father's law, pronounces the patriarchal sentence on the matriarchal chorus: the women will withdraw to a subterranean cavern where they will be permitted to establish a cult, perform religious rites and sacrifices, and remain "loyal and propitious to the land." They are removed from positions of influence, their words destined to have only subterranean meaning.

Therefore, the narrator speaks the law of the father in the form of a "women's language" which is prescribed by patriarchy and exacts its sentence upon her: not to author sentences of her own.

The yellow wallpaper challenges this sentence. In contrast to the orderly, evacuated patriarchal estate, the female lineage that the wallpaper represents is thick with life, expression, and suffering. Masquerading as a symptom of "madness," language animates what had been merely an irritating and distracting pattern:

> This paper looks to me as if it *knew* what a vicious influence it had!
> There is a recurrent spot where the pattern lolls like a broken neck and two bulbous eyes stare at you upside down.
> I get positively angry with the impertinence of it and the everlastingness.
> Up and down and sideways they crawl, and those absurd, unblinking eyes are everywhere. (16)

The silly and grotesque surface pattern reflects women's conventional representation; one juxtaposition identifies "that silly and conspicuous front design" with "sister on the stairs!" (18). In the middle section of the story, where the narrator attempts to convey her belief that she is seriously ill, the husband–physician is quoted verbatim (23–25), enabling us to see the operation of male judgment at first hand. He notes an improvement in her symptoms: "You are gaining flesh and color, your appetite is better, I feel really much easier about you." The narrator disputes these statements: "I don't weigh a bit more, nor as much; and my appetite may be better in the evening when you are here, but it is worse in the morning when you are away!" His response not only pre-empts further talk of facts, it reinforces the certainty of his original diagnosis and confirms his view of her illness as non-serious: "'Bless her little heart!' said he with a big hug, 'she shall be as sick as she pleases!'" (24).

His failure to let her leave the estate initiates a new relationship to the wallpaper. She begins to see women in the pattern. Until now, we as readers have acquiesced in the fiction that the protagonist is keeping a journal, a fiction initially supported by journal-like textual references. This now becomes difficult to sustain: how can the narrator keep a journal when, as she tells us, she is sleeping, creeping, or watching the wallpaper the whole time? In her growing paranoia, would she confide in a journal she could not lock up? How did the journal get into our hands? Because we are nevertheless reading this "journal," we are forced to experience a contradiction: the narrative is unfolding in an impossible form. This embeds our experience of the story in self-conscious attention to its construction. A new tone enters as she reports that she defies orders to take naps by not actually sleeping: "And that cultivates deceit, for I don't tell them I'm awake—O no!" (26). This crowing tone announces a decisive break from the patriarchal order. She mocks her husband's diagnosis by diagnosing for herself why he "seems very queer sometimes": "It strikes me occasionally, just as a scientific hypothesis,—that perhaps it is the paper!" (26–27).

The wallpaper never becomes attractive. It remains indeterminate, complex, unresolved, disturbing; it continues to embody, like the form of the story we are reading, "unheard of contradictions." By now the narrator is fully engrossed by it and determined to find out its meaning. During the day—by "normal" standards—it remains "tiresome and perplexing" (28). But at night she sees a woman, or many women, shaking the pattern and trying to climb through it. Women "get through," she perceives, "and then the pattern strangles them off and turns them upside down, and makes their eyes white!" (30). The death sentence imposed by patriarchy is violent and relentless. No one escapes.

The story is now at its final turning point: "I have found out another funny thing," reports the narrator, "but I shan't tell it this time! It does not do to trust people too much" (31). This is a break with patriarchy—and a break with us. What she has discovered, which she does not state, is that she and the woman behind the paper are the same. This is communicated syntactically by contrasting sentences: "This bedstead is fairly gnawed!" she tells us, and then: "I bit off a little piece (of the bedstead) at one corner" (34). "If that woman does get out, and tries to get away, I can tie her!" and "But I am securely fastened now by my well-hidden rope" (34–35). The final passages are filled with crowing, "impertinent" language: "Hurrah!" "The sly thing!" "No person touches this paper but me,—not *alive!*" (32–33). Locked in the room, she addresses her husband in a dramatically different way: "It is no use, young man, you can't open it!"

She does not make this declaration aloud. In fact, she appears to have difficulty even making herself understood and must repeat several times the instructions to her husband for finding the key to the room. At first we think she may be too mad to speak proper English. But then we realize that he simply is unable to accept a statement of fact from her, his little goose, until she has "said it so often that he had to go and see" (36). Her final triumph is her public proclamation, "I've got out at last . . . you can't put me back!" (36).

There is a dramatic shift here both in *what* is said and in *who* is speaking. Not only has a new "impertinent" self emerged, but this final voice is collective, representing the narrator, the woman behind the wallpaper, and women elsewhere and everywhere. The final vision itself is one of physical enslavement, not liberation: the woman, bound by a rope, circles the room like an animal in a yoke. Yet that this vision has come to exist and to be expressed changes the terms of the representational process. That the husband–physician must at last listen to a woman speaking—no matter what she says—significantly changes conditions for speaking. Though patriarchy may be only temporarily unconscious, its ancestral halls will never be precisely the same again.

We can return now to the questions raised at the outset. Language in "The Yellow Wallpaper" is oppressive to women in the particular form of a medical diagnosis, a set of linguistic signs whose representational claims are authorized by society and whose power to control women's fate, whether or not those claims are valid, is real. Representation has real, material consequences. In contrast, women's power to originate signs is monitored; and, once produced, no legitimating social apparatus is available to give those signs substance in the real world.

Linguistic innovation, then, has a dual fate. The narrator in "The Yellow Wallpaper" initially speaks a language authorized by patriarchy, with genuine language ("work") forbidden her. But as the wallpaper comes alive she devises a different, "impertinent" language which defies patriarchal control and confounds the predictions of male judgment (diagnosis). The fact that she becomes a creative and involved language user, producing sentences which break established rules, *in and of itself* changes the terms in which women are represented in language and extends the conditions under which women will speak.

Yet language is intimately connected to material reality, despite the fact that no direct correspondence exists. The word is theory to the deed: but the deed's existence will depend upon a complicated set of material conditions. The narrator of "The Yellow Wallpaper" is not free at the end of the story because she has temporarily escaped her sentence: though she has "got out at last," her triumph is to have sharpened and articulated the nature of women's condition; she remains physically bound by a rope and locked in a room. The conditions she has diagnosed must change before she and other women will be free. Thus women's control of language is left metaphorical and evocative: the story only hints at possibilities for change. Woman is both passive and active, subject and object, sane and mad. Contradictions remain, for they are inherent in women's current "condition."

Thus to "escape the sentence" involves both linguistic innovation and change in material conditions: both change in what is said and change in the conditions of speaking. The escape of individual women may constitute a kind of linguistic self-help which has intrinsic value as a contribution to language but which functions socially and politically to isolate deviance rather than to introduce change. Representation is not without consequence. The study of women and language must involve the study of discourse, which encompasses both form and function as well as the representational uncertainty their relationship entails. As a metaphor, the yellow wallpaper is never fully resolved: it can be described, but its meaning cannot be fixed. It remains trivial and dramatic, vivid and dowdy, compelling and repulsive: these multiple meanings run throughout the story in contrast to the one certain meaning of patriarchal diagnosis. If diagnosis is the middle of an equation that freezes material flux in a certain sign, the wallpaper is a disruptive center that chaotically fragments any attempt to fix on it a single meaning. It offers a lesson in language, whose sentence is perhaps not always destined to escape us.

CATHERINE GOLDEN

"Overwriting" the Rest Cure:
Charlotte Perkins Gilman's Literary
Escape from S. Weir Mitchell's
Fictionalization of Women
(1992)

In 1887 S. Weir Mitchell treated Charlotte Perkins Gilman (then Stetson)[1] for a nervous breakdown following a postpartum depression and forbade her to write.[2] A specialist in women's nervous disorders, Mitchell attended well-known male and female literary figures. George Meredith and Walt Whitman apparently experienced no ill effects from his prescriptions; Jane Addams, Edith Wharton, Charlotte Perkins Gilman, and Virginia Woolf

---

[1] Gilman was then Charlotte Perkins Stetson. She also published "The Yellow Wallpaper" under that name. For consistency, this article refers to her throughout as Gilman.

[2] Gilman discusses S. Weir Mitchell's full prescription following her Rest Cure treatment in her autobiography, *The Living of Charlotte Perkins Gilman: An Autobiography* (New York: D. Appleton-Century, 1935), 96; hereafter cited as *Living*.

suffered from his Rest Cure treatment.[3] After nearly losing her sanity by rigidly following his parting advice "never [to] touch pen, brush or pencil as long as you live" (*Living*, 96), Gilman defied Mitchell and transformed him into a minor but memorable character in her fiction. In "The Yellow Wallpaper" the nameless narrator, undergoing a three-month Rest Cure for a postpartum depression, protests that her physician/husband John "says if I don't pick up faster he shall send me to Weir Mitchell in the fall."[4] Although Gilman does not discuss her physician in detail in her story, she does name him as well as indict him in this one salient reference, which continues: "But I don't want to go there at all. I had a friend who was in his hands once, and she says he is just like John and my brother, only more so!" (19).

Gilman's introduction of her doctor into a first-person narrative gains interest and complexity when we consider that this foremost nineteenth-century American neurologist had a second career as a novelist. In addition to medical books and essays on the nervous system, mental fatigue, and convalescence, he published several collections of short stories, three volumes of poetry, and nineteen novels between 1884 and 1913.[5] Although virtually

---

[3] George Meredith was pleased with the results of a buttermilk diet S. Weir Mitchell had recommended, and he was enthusiastic about Mitchell's fiction; he considered *Roland Blake* Mitchell's best novel. Mitchell treated Walt Whitman occasionally and gave him funds to help him to continue writing. Suzanne Poirier notes, however, that "Mitchell's treatment of Jane Addams, Winifred Howells (daughter of William Dean Howells), and Charlotte Perkins Gilman, and the use of his treatment on Virginia Woolf caused cries of protest from all these women and their families" (15). Although Woolf never saw Mitchell, a British neurologist, Dr. Playfair, brought the Weir Mitchell Rest Cure to England in 1880 and encouraged its use. The treatment Woolf's physician, Dr. Savage, prescribed following her second breakdown in 1904 included a milk regimen, rest, and isolation. Although Woolf did not completely reject the treatment, she complained bitterly about it to friends and attacked it through her fiction such as *Mrs. Dalloway* (1925). In 1898 Edith Wharton traveled to Mitchell's sanitarium in Philadelphia to seek Mitchell's care. Her treatment was more moderate: not hospitalized, she remained in a hotel room and was allowed to write letters; however, she had enforced bed rest and was permitted no visitors for four months. For more information on Mitchell's treatment of male and female literary figures, see Suzanne Poirier, "The Weir Mitchell Rest Cure: Doctor and Patients," *Women's Studies Quarterly* 10, no. 1 (1983): 15–40. For more discussion of Mitchell's relationship with Meredith and Whitman, see Ernest Earnest, *S. Weir Mitchell: Novelist and Physician* (Philadelphia: University of Pennsylvania Press, 1950), 40, 99–100, 115; hereafter cited as Earnest.

[4] Charlotte Perkins Gilman, *The Yellow Wallpaper* (Old Westbury: Feminist Press, 1973), 18; hereafter cited in the text.

[5] The *Definitive Edition* of S. Weir Mitchell's oeuvre amounts to 6500 pages. The exact number of his short story volumes and novels remains unknown because he destroyed several of these works before they were actually published.

unknown today, Mitchell was, in fact, one of the most popular turn-of-the-century American writers; critics compared Mitchell's *Hugh Wynne* (1896) to Thackeray's *Henry Esmond* (1852).[6] Many of his literary efforts incorporated psychiatric themes and doctor-patient relationships informed by his own practice and that of his affluent physician father, John Kearsley Mitchell.

Supporters of Mitchell's fiction such as David Rein and Ernest Earnest argue that Mitchell "deserves to be restored to the canon of American literature" (Earnest, 235).[7] Rein praises Mitchell as an author, for "in his fictional studies of nervous disorders he stood alone. He was the first novelist in American literature to present such clinically accurate portraits of mentally ill characters. No one else had done it, except Oliver Wendell Holmes. But even Holmes's work lacks much of the merit of Mitchell's" (Rein, 182–83). However, even those who commend Mitchell's fictional studies modeled after his own patients are quick to raise his shortcomings as a novelist. Mitchell's fiction disappoints because it often fails to bring a character vividly to life, to explore the causes of the protagonists' nervous breakdowns, or to show their progressive deterioration into hysteria, as Rein and Jeffrey Berman have noted.[8] Moreover, as a writer, Mitchell sacrifices the plotline of his novels to feature conversations his characters have with one another; as a result, his style is conversational at best.

Mitchell never wrote about Gilman in his fiction exploring abnormal psychology or in his psychiatric books detailing the Weir Mitchell Rest Cure. Nonetheless, his almost forgotten fiction offers insight into why Gilman decided to write "The Yellow Wallpaper"; in her words, "to reach Dr. S. Weir Mitchell, and convince him of the error of his ways" (*Living*, 121). A comparison of the fictional female characters in S. Weir Mitchell's

---

[6] *Hugh Wynne* sold over one-half million copies and is often regarded as Mitchell's best book. In the foreword to *S. Weir Mitchell: Novelist and Physician,* Ernest Earnest writes that Mitchell's *"Hugh Wynne* was compared to *Henry Esmond,* his *Ode on a Lycian Tomb* to *Lycidas."* Jeffrey Berman also makes this point in "The Unrestful Cure: Charlotte Perkins Gilman and 'The Yellow Wallpaper,'" *The Talking Cure: Literary Representations of Psychoanalysis* (New York: New York University Press, 1985), 48; hereafter cited as Berman.

[7] David Rein similarly states: "Mitchell's novels should be evaluated anew, for his accomplishments deserve to be recalled more widely and wrought into the tradition of American culture" (*S. Weir Mitchell as a Psychiatric Novelist* [New York: International Universities Press, 1952], 202); hereafter cited as Rein.

[8] See Berman, 45–49, and Rein, 186–202. Berman's essay cites this important connection and discusses the range of Mitchell's fiction; however, his chapter does not explore the relationship between Gilman's fiction and Mitchell's.

late nineteenth-century novels and Gilman's own protagonist in "The Yellow Wallpaper" (1892) suggests that through his Rest Cure treatment Mitchell tried to reform his patient Charlotte Perkins Gilman along the lines of his fictional female protagonists, many of whom followed a version of his Rest Cure. Mitchell's *Characteristics* (1891), written shortly after Gilman's treatment in Mitchell's sanitarium, demonstrates the physician/author's patriarchal portrayal of the (male) doctor-(female) patient relationship that Gilman revised in "The Yellow Wallpaper" (1892). She defied her doctor in 1890 not only by writing "The Yellow Wallpaper" but also, more specifically, by creating a protagonist who also writes. Her creative life and her fiction reveal that she ultimately "overwrote" Mitchell's efforts to make her more like the ideal female patients predominant in his affluent medical practice and his fiction.

Gilman was twenty-six years old when she traveled to Philadelphia to enter the sanitarium of Dr. S. Weir Mitchell. Like Sigmund Freud, Mitchell was trained as a neurologist, but he earned special recognition as a nerve specialist for women. Only by the end of the century did the medical profession, influenced by the work of Freud, begin to distinguish between diseases of the mind, to be treated by psychiatrists, and diseases of the brain, to be treated by neurologists. Neurology in the mid-to-late nineteenth century explored the relationship between psychology and physiology. Nerves were considered the link between the mind and the body, and the symptoms of mental exhaustion and depression were thought to be somatic in origin. Aiming to heal the mind by healing the body, Mitchell's Rest Cure attended to the physical symptoms of depression. Although Mitchell is credited with the Rest Cure, he developed it from a number of accepted medical practices. His Rest Cure earned him international acclaim (his work was translated into four languages before his death in 1914). In fact, Freud favorably reviewed Mitchell's first book, *Fat and Blood* (1877), approved of his Rest Cure, and even adapted and used it for a period of time.[9]

---

[9] Earnest, 227, and Regina Markell Morantz, "The Perils of Feminist History," *Women and Health in America*, ed. Judith Walzer Leavitt (Madison: University of Wisconsin Press, 1984), 239–45. In her criticism of Ann Douglas Wood's essay, "'The Fashionable Diseases': Women's Complaints and Their Treatment in Nineteenth-Century America," *The Journal of Interdisciplinary History* 4 (1973): 25–52, Morantz offers a much more favorable reading of S. Weir Mitchell than Wood, Poirier, and Gilman's biographer Ann J. Lane, author of *To Herland and Beyond: The Life and Work of Charlotte Perkins Gilman* (New York: Pantheon Books, 1990); hereafter cited as Lane. Perturbed that Mitchell's personality "is so utterly distorted in Wood's characterization" (240), Morantz rebuts specific claims that Wood

Mitchell diagnosed Gilman's condition as "nervous prostration" or "neurasthenia," a breakdown of the nervous system, and prescribed his Rest Cure. Following the birth of her daughter, she had become depressed, spiritless, weak, and hysterical. This psychiatric condition was in no way unique to Gilman or to the female population; men also suffered from it, as had Mitchell himself.[10] Because of the strains on the Victorian woman imposed by the rigid ideals of femininity, debilitating nervous disorders were more common among upper- and middle-class women than men. The causes of neurasthenia were thought to be gender-specific: while men succumbed from overwork, women suffered from too much social activity, sustained or severe domestic trials (e.g., nursing a sick family member), and overexertion brought on by pursuing higher education.

In treating his patients Mitchell demanded obedience and deliberately assumed a detached, stern manner that he believed helpful, especially for patients who had been pampered and indulged by well-intentioned relatives. He was patronizing to women, a trend that characterizes his extensive writing about the Rest Cure, mental fatigue, and convalescence. For instance, in *Doctor and Patient,* Mitchell writes that "there are many kinds of fool, from the mindless fool to the fiend-fool, but for the most entire capacity to make a household wretched there is no more complete human receipt than a silly woman who is to a high degree nervous and feeble, and who craves pity and likes power";[11] in fact, he considered Gilman's involvement in the history of her own case "proved self-conceit" (*Living,* 95). Nonetheless, Mitchell was more liberal than many male physicians of his time. He believed in the legitimacy of and the suffering caused by neurasthenia, validating women's complaints. He openly scorned the abuse of ovariotomies and other forms

---

makes in her essay: that Mitchell believed that women doctors would always be inferior to male doctors, that doctors were gods, and that patients were to be docile children. She presents Mitchell as a neurologist, not a "woman's doctor" as Wood does; she also discusses the effective use of his treatment on soldiers suffering from battle fatigue as well as the praise Mitchell received from Freud.

10   Although Mitchell initially earned his reputation during the Civil War for his treatment of gunshot victims suffering from paralysis, he came to specialize in nervous diseases, which had plagued him as a young man. His first nervous breakdown occurred just after the Civil War, following the death of his young wife and his affluent Virginia physician father (who had initially opposed his decision to enter medicine); his second breakdown came three years after in 1872, following the death of his mother.

11   S. Weir Mitchell, *Doctor and Patient* (Philadelphia: Lippincott, 1888), 117.

of commonly prescribed radical gynecological surgery. Mitchell also approved of physical exercise as well as higher education for women in the areas of child care and home management in order to fit women for the domestic sphere.[12]

Although Mitchell's Rest Cure was in accordance with the most advanced neurological thinking of his day, in modern eyes it can be read as an attempt to reorient women to the domestic sphere (and away from influences of their changing world) so that they could fulfill their most important role in society: to bear and rear children. The covert aim of severely enforcing the treatment was so that the patient would feel "surfeited with [rest] and [would] welcome a firm order to do the things she once felt she could not do."[13] Typically lasting six to eight weeks, the Rest Cure focused on nutrition and revitalization of the body. It included five components: total, enforced, extended bed rest (the patient was forbidden to sew, converse, move herself in and out of bed, read, write, and, in more extreme cases, even to feed herself); seclusion from family and familiar surroundings (to remove the patient from the pampering of well-meaning relatives would sever hurtful old habits); a carefully controlled diet (overfeeding, the key ingredient being milk and cream to create new energy by increasing body volume); massage; and electricity (the latter two components were introduced to prevent muscular atrophy).[14]

The Rest Cure was not without merits; similar to the spa water cures in fashion in nineteenth-century Europe and America, the Rest Cure removed the individual from the tensions of his or her world and offered a sanctuary for rest. Hundreds of women traveled to Mitchell's sanitarium from around the world to seek his Rest Cure. Many felt relieved that their complaints had been both recognized and treated, and they left satisfied. Nonetheless, to many women, including Gilman, Mitchell's Rest Cure was punitive. Mitchell admitted that his methods of treating women for neurasthenia were harsh: "Rest can be made to help. Rest can also hurt."[15] Despite this

---

[12] S. Weir Mitchell, *Wear and Tear* (Philadelphia: Lippincott, 1871), 33.

[13] S. Weir Mitchell, quoted in Lane, 117.

[14] Mitchell did not anticipate that his female patients, under treatment, would continue to question and apply their creative minds as was the case with Gilman, who followed his treatment for one month.

[15] S. Weir Mitchell, "Rest in Nervous Disease: Its Use and Abuse," *A Series of American Clinical Lectures*, ed. E. C. Sequin, M.D., 1(1875): 102.

admission of what many women feared about his Rest Cure, Mitchell consistently defended his methods as necessary to cure them, allowing them to resume their traditional domestic roles.

Threatened by the direction of the "new woman" emerging in the late nineteenth century, Mitchell clung to the traditional view of the dutiful, protected woman and immortalized her in his fiction. Unlike the women in Gilman's stories, passive heroines abound in Mitchell's writings. Some female characters demonstrate intellectual vigor, such as Alice Leigh in *Characteristics,* or exert strong will, such as Serena Vernon in *A Comedy of Conscience* (1900). Both ultimately put aside their independent notions and follow the advice of strong male characters, taking the opposite course from that of Gilman's protagonists.

At least in the novel's opening, *A Comedy of Conscience* reveals a portrait of a liberated woman. A spinster by choice, Serena is described as a healthy, attractive, strong-willed, and "intelligent, but not intellectual"[16] woman who often asks for but seldom takes advice. Similar to the nameless protagonist in "The Yellow Wallpaper," Serena keeps a diary throughout the novel and has a suitor named John (a common name in Mitchell's fiction).[17] While the nameless protagonist in "The Yellow Wallpaper" defies her husband/physician John, Serena Vernon increasingly relies on her male cousin John Winterbourne, her rejected suitor who remains devoted to her. Serena becomes more dependent upon others for advice after she is robbed—a criminal steals her wallet on the trolley-car (and inadvertently drops a stolen diamond ring into her handbag); although Mitchell does not overtly discuss the robbery as a cause of her change, this event seemingly accounts for Serena's dramatic transformation from self-sufficiency to dependency on the advice of male figures, namely the trusted Doctor Saffron, her rector, and John. Although Serena asks advice of her "nearest female friend" (8) Mrs. Clare regarding what to do with the "stolen" diamond ring and even claims "A woman will see this miserable business from my side" (41), she discounts Mrs. Clare's advice; she listens instead to John, whose hand in marriage she accepts at the very end of the novel (despite her strong convictions not to marry him at the beginning). At this point, Serena's John

---

[16] S. Weir Mitchell, *A Comedy of Conscience* (New York: The Century Co., 1903), 8; hereafter cited in the text.

[17] John was also S. Weir Mitchell's father's name and his son's name. Although the choice of name for the male protagonist in Mitchell's and Gilman's fiction may be merely coincidental, *Characteristics* was published prior to "The Yellow Wallpaper."

declares her "nervous" (although we were initially assured that she was rarely ill) and prescribes rest: "Go to bed, dear" (125). When she resists, he calls her a "Dear child!" (127), paternalistic language reminiscent of the nameless protagonist's husband John in "The Yellow Wallpaper."

In an earlier novel, *Roland Blake* (1886), the most interesting character is not the hero Roland, an intelligence officer in the Union army, but a more minor character, Octopia Darnell, a patient similar to those Mitchell describes again and again in *Doctor and Patient* and *Fat and Blood*.[18] Octopia—who shuns the light, constantly complains, and prefers to recline rather than stand—is thin and lacks blood. By giving Octopia an attenuated frame and impoverished blood, Mitchell embodies in his fictional patient two of the outstanding characteristics of the class of nervous women for whom he devised and prescribed his Rest Cure.[19] At the onset of the novel, Octopia is a "settled inmate"[20] in the home of a distant relative, the elderly Mrs. Wynne. The cause of her physical condition, which we are told has no physiological origin, remains unclear until the second third of the novel. Nursing Mrs. Wynne's son, Arthur, during the last week of his life, Octopia witnesses his suicide and immediately proclaims herself ill. She gains power over Mrs. Wynne by declaring that her illness results from the strain of attending Arthur Wynne at his deathbed and by threatening to reveal Arthur's suicide (her recovery would thus diminish her claim on Mrs. Wynne).

Arthur Wynne's daughter, Olivia, comes to live in the home of her paternal grandmother, in which her distant invalid cousin Octopia has earned a permanent residence. With Olivia's arrival, the hysterical Octopia, whom Mitchell describes as "too wicked to die" (62), becomes a scheming chronic invalid who assigns herself to bed but continues to use her invalid status to plague her younger, passive cousin Olivia (e.g., "'That was rough child. You forget I am an invalid'" [44]); she also tyrannizes Mrs. Wynne (e.g., "She [Octopia] is killing me by inches" [62]), who fears Octopia too much to remove her from her own home. Throughout the novel Olivia defers to her petulant, selfish, and cunning older cousin and becomes nursemaid both to her elderly grandmother and Octopia.

---

[18] Rein also makes this point and argues, "While the main story [of *Roland Blake*] is about quite normal people, the main attraction is in the abnormal minor characters" (Rein, 190). Octopia, however, is not as minor a character as he implies.

[19] Mitchell describes these women in *Fat and Blood* as "nervous women, who as a rule are thin and lack blood" (Philadelphia: Lippincott, 1878), 7; hereafter cited in the text.

[20] S. Weir Mitchell, *Roland Blake* (New York: The Century Co., 1901), 40; hereafter cited in the text.

Mitchell does not glorify Octopia's well-meaning "victim" (97) but uses Olivia to make a point in fiction central to his medical writings on the Rest Cure: the overindulgence of well-intentioned relatives can only exacerbate the hysterical patient's condition and weaken the caretaker's health. In Olivia's case, "the exactions of her nervous, sickly cousin were surely sapping the wholesome life of the younger woman, and as surely lessening her power of self-restraint" (50). The forbearing Olivia, whose health deteriorates, admits that the capricious Octopia is only "half-sick": "what must be the worst evil of half-sick people is the absence of regular work, of set duties—things that must be done" (376). However, Octopia, like many of the hysterically ill women Mitchell treated in his practice, does not know she is cruel to others: "she thought about herself and thought she didn't think about herself" (376). At the end of the novel, Mitchell rewards Olivia with marriage to Roland Blake and frees her from her nursemaid position. Olivia's departure, compounded by Mrs. Wynne's death, leads Octopia to wed Addenda Pennell, who caters to her whims as Olivia once did (e.g., "As for Pennell, he followed her [Octopia] about with a shawl and a scent-bottle, and says he has left the club and prefers the evening tranquility of domestic life" [379]). Mitchell is too much a realist to reform Octopia or to restore her health. Rather, this final twist shows how both sexes can succumb to the tyranny of the kind of "half-sick" patient possessing "the most entire capacity to make a household wretched" that Mitchell bemoans in *Doctor and Patient* and his other medical writings.[21]

An apparent exception to the undermining of women's initiative by male (typically the physician's) authority occurs in *Constance Trescot* (1905). The eponymous heroine avenges the unjust death of her lawyer/husband George Trescot, who was shot by an emotionally unstable lawyer named Greyhurst under the pretense of a duel. Constance's power and authority, however, are only seen to serve male authority: these traits allow her to ruin her husband's murderer and to restore George Trescot's name and reputation. In other respects, Constance behaves like a typical Mitchell hysteric. Predictably, at the scene of the murder, Constance falls "insensible, convulsed, and quivering" at her husband's murderer's feet.[22] Although a physically healthy woman at the opening of the novel, her passionate and obsessive

---

[21] In *Fat and Blood*, Mitchell describes this relationship and concludes "the nurse falls ill, and a new victim is found. I have seen an hysterical, anaemic girl kill in this way three generations of nurses" (30).

[22] S. Weir Mitchell, *Constance Trescot* (New York: The Century Co., 1909), 222; hereafter cited in the text.

love for her husband (which lies beyond the scope of Mitchell's inquiry) triggers an emotional collapse that leaves her physically wasted and eventually turns her into an anemic, "couch-loving invalid,"[23] rivaling Octopia Darnell. She devotes her life to ruining Greyhurst (who is not found guilty of murder) and uses her disabled status to rule her caretakers (e.g., "Constance relied on her misfortunes and her long illness to insure her an excess of sympathetic affection and unremitting service" [382]). In fact, just as Octopia made Olivia the victim of her demands in *Roland Blake*, Constance expects her well-meaning sister Susan to care for her tirelessly and, like Octopia, seems unaware of her own selfish nature.[24]

Unlike *Roland Blake* and *Constance Trescot*, which offer portraits of tiresome invalids whose conditions worsen due to the indulgence of well-intentioned relatives, *Characteristics* and its sequel, *Dr. North and His Friends* (1900), epitomize the relationship between the (male) doctor and the ideal (female) patient that Mitchell prescribes and Gilman defies in the literary arena.[25] Two parts of the same story, these semiautobiographical novels of conversation contain developed characters but do not have a sustained plot. Both works, narrated by Dr. Owen North, offer veiled self-portraits of Mitchell's own life; this is particularly true of *Characteristics*, which describes North's war injuries (Mitchell himself suffered greatly from the Civil War) and his ambivalence about pursuing medicine (Mitchell battled with his father, who initially objected to his career choice). Both novels feature female patients and offer but one strong female protagonist; Anne Vincent, the

---

23. Rein uses this term to describe Octopia Darnell in *Roland Blake*, Constance Trescot in *Constance Trescot*, and Ann Penhallow in *Westways* (1914), Mitchell's last novel. See his chapter "The Couch-Loving Invalids."

24. Susan in *Constance Trescot*, like Olivia in *Roland Blake*, escapes her ministering role through marriage, and Constance goes abroad with a nursemaid.

25. These novels were not well reviewed as some of Mitchell's other fiction. The *Nation* called *Characteristics* "not very exciting" but recognized that it was "sane and even in tone" ("More Novels," *Nation* 55 [8 December 1892], 437). The style of *Dr. North and His Friends* received more stringent criticism: "Almost everybody who believes himself to be intelligent may be heard, at one time or another, expressing a regret that the age of conversation is past. An attempt to read the conversations between 'Dr. North and His Friends' is likely to stifle such regrets; indeed, to convert them into an ardent prayer that the art may not be revived, at least in our time" ("Recent Novels," *Nation* 72 [28 February 1901], 182). The book was better received by the *Critic*, which called *Dr. North and His Friends* "a book such as only a wise and learned man could write, for it garners the wit and wisdom of a lifetime" ("Fiction," *Critic* 37 [January 1901], 86). For more discussion of these and other works, see Rein, particularly his concluding chapter entitled "Mitchell as a Novelist" (178–202).

wife of Dr. North's best friend, Frederick Vincent, stands out as an intelligent and intrusive social matron, yet her strong role as a female adviser is undermined by Mitchell's frequent references to her unfortunate childless state. Both works offer Mitchell an occasion to present his belief that women can be good patients but not necessarily successful doctors.

In *Fat and Blood*, Mitchell states that women doctors "do not obtain the needed control over those of their own sex" (41). Mitchell questioned whether women doctors could exert the strict, objective manner necessary to manage the class of hysterical invalids that his fictional characters Octopia Darnell and Constance Trescot represent. Of course, in *Fat and Blood* he also admits that the male physician may also experience difficulty with this type of patient, and he does refer in passing to the abilities of women physicians as he qualifies: "it is in these cases that women who are in all other cases capable doctors fail" (41).[26] More than by the issue of competence, Mitchell was disturbed by the personal consequences for women entering medicine. Through the development of Alice Leigh in *Characteristics*, he presents his belief that a "capable" woman doctor would lose her essential femininity.

While the nameless protagonist in "The Yellow Wallpaper" defies her physician/husband John as the story continues, Alice Leigh enters the story as a woman with a mind and will of her own who sacrifices her convictions to follow the ideas of Dr. Owen North, who speaks Mitchell's views. Anne Vincent initially describes Alice as "a woman of unusual force of character . . . and intellect (for she is more than merely intelligent)."[27] Her quality of mind at the outset of the novel surpasses that of Serena Vernon's in *A Comedy of Conscience*. Mrs. Leigh, Alice's mother, turns to the much-respected Dr. North for advice when she discovers the extent of her daughter's ambitions: "Now she [Alice] proposes to . . . it is awful. She wants to study medicine, and, oh, you do not know Alice. She is so determined" (235). Owen North shares Mrs. Leigh's belief that a woman's entrance into the medical profession is "awful." Though initially "determined" to pursue "something which offers an enlarging life" (249), Alice rather quickly abandons her plans to study and practice medicine right after Dr. North prescribes otherwise.

---

26 This point has been much debated between Wood and Morantz; while Wood claims that Mitchell believes "women doctors would always be inferior to male physicians" in "'The Fashionable Diseases'" (228), Morantz finds no firm support for this claim in *Fat and Blood* or any of Mitchell's writings (240).

27 S. Weir Mitchell, *Characteristics* (New York: The Century Co., 1891), 234; hereafter cited in the text.

Although Owen does not attend Alice for a physical malady, her plan to be a doctor is referred to as a "disease" (235), and North counsels her as he would his female patients. When she first meets Owen North, the twenty-four-year-old Alice passionately ridicules her mother's suggestions that she sketch, play music, and sew. Spirited Alice argues for the need for "an enlarging life" (249), not for personal ambition but to benefit her society. Owen wins Alice's favor when he professes that "every human being is entitled to any career he or she may please to desire" (251); however, he soon reveals his prejudices. He tells Alice: "I said I did not believe it was best either for the sick or for society for women to be doctors; that, personally, women lose something of the natural charm of their sex in giving themselves either to this or to the other avocations until now in the sole possession of a man" (264). Immediately following their discussion, Alice becomes "quite tranquil" (275) and acquiesces to her mother's plan to leave behind her "'hunger for imperative duties'" (235) and concentrate on marriage. Unfortunately, Mitchell neither explores nor explains the cause of Alice's sudden transformation, which seems implausible to the contemporary reader.

When Alice suddenly becomes ill (she starts looking pale), Mrs. Leigh attempts to engage Owen North as Alice's physician. He refuses because he has fallen in love with her. Proposing to Alice on the penultimate page of the novel, Owen secures the hand of the once willful Alice, who has become so rattled that she shreds her fan in a dozen bits as she accepts his proposal. Reduced to tears, she "sobbed like a child" and admits defeat: "Owen North, be very good to me. I meant to have done so much" (306). Rather than become a doctor, she marries the man who advises her not to develop her intellect. Mitchell concludes that, Alice, like her mother before her, is "cured" of her ambitions by marriage (235). At the end of the novel, Alice represents the ideals Mitchell prescribes to women through his medical writings and in his fiction. Nonetheless, the tearful state of the obedient Alice testifies to the trauma she experiences in putting aside her desire for a purposeful career only to gain usefulness through her physician/husband's life.

The narrator in "The Yellow Wallpaper" also sobs uncontrollably, although primarily at the beginning of the story.[28] Gilman revises the typical (male) doctor-(female) patient relationship by reversing the heroine's progress: Mitchell's strong-willed Alice is made passive, whereas Gilman's once submissive protagonist gains a forceful sense of self as she acts out of

---

[28] While Mitchell's females typically cry in front of their physicians, Gilman's narrator conceals her sobbing.

madness. Initially Gilman's nameless protagonist is as obedient to her physician/husband John as Mitchell's Alice Leigh sadly becomes toward her future husband/physician Owen North. Gilman's narrator defers to "Dear John" as well as to what "John says" (16) when he prescribes Mitchell's Rest Cure. Even though her room initially repulses her, she rests in the former nursery because John chose it for her. She stops her writing when she senses John's entry.

In her own text Gilman creates through the characterization of John a physician of "high standing" (10) who is also self-assured ("I am a doctor, dear, and I know" [23]) and thus similar to Owen North and to Mitchell himself. Moreover, John's authority is backed by the protagonist's well-respected physician/brother and by the threat of S. Weir Mitchell "only more so" (19). Unlike Mitchell's Alice, Gilman's heroine becomes aware of her submissiveness and defies her doctor's advice. Referring and deferring less to John as the story continues, the narrator pursues her ambitions: first, to find out the pattern of the wallpaper, then to tear it away, freeing the woman (and that part of herself) trapped behind the pattern. As she creeps along the walls of the sanitarium/prison, her actions move beyond the realm of sanity. Nonetheless, acting out of madness, she defies John and the male-dominated medical profession he represents. She creeps flamboyantly in the daytime as she desires. While Alice Leigh rips her fan to bits and acquiesces to her physician/husband, the nameless protagonist in "The Yellow Wallpaper" creeps over her physician/husband—a crucial reversal. Although her mad state allows her only a dubious victory,[29] in Gilman's story it is the male physician whose force is circumvented and who faints when confronted by the newly claimed autonomy of his female patient.

The behavior of Gilman's narrator also diverges from that of the female protagonists in *Dr. North and His Friends,* the sequel to *Characteristics.* This novel confirms the total submission of Alice Leigh, for whom even a dubious victory never comes. The narrator of *Dr. North and His Friends* refers to the once independent Alice Leigh as Mrs. North or "my wife." Throughout this novel, Alice's voice is silenced as a result of her constant deference to her husband/physician. Now unsure of her intellectual abilities, Alice Leigh

---

[29] The end of Gilman's controversial story invites conflicting interpretations of entrapment and liberation. While many critics read the conclusion as a triumph, some argue that she is defeated, and others assert that she achieves a partial victory. For further reading on this range of interpretations, see *The Captive Imagination: A Casebook on "The Yellow Wallpaper,"* ed. Catherine Golden. (New York: Feminist Press, 1991).

relies on her husband to supply her with knowledge and support during social conversations: "I never can express what I mean. Sometimes I think I am clever, but when I talk it out I conclude that I am a fool. Tell me what I mean." [30] Frequently her discussions of social issues are flavored with her husband's paternalistic views. Although she once fervently wished to be a doctor, Alice radically alters her perception of a woman's aptitude for medicine and comes to hold her husband's—and Mitchell's—belief that a woman should solely be educated in the area of domestic duties. Her friend Sibyl Maywood, a memorable invalid in Mitchell's fiction, shares this view and voices Mitchell's belief in a woman doctor's inability to exert control: "I do not think I should like to have a woman doctor. . . . Oh, I should never obey her—never; why, I could not say. I should have no confidence" (127).

Sibyl Maywood enters Dr. North's circle when North's friend Xerxes Claybourne hires his cousin Sibyl as his secretary to aid him in his scholarship. Sibyl has a physical disability that becomes the subject of much conversation throughout the novel. Victor St. Clair, the free-spirited, attractive bachelor artist, says: "She is lame and not quite erect" (34). Claybourne explains apologetically: "She is slightly, very slightly deformed, and halts" (35). Using more graphic, clinical terms, Owen North laments that Sibyl has a "maimed body" (76). One shoulder is slightly higher than the other, and she walks in a halting gait, but "above this crooked frame rose a head of the utmost beauty" (42). Anne Vincent regrets that Sibyl is not also "deformed of face" (35) because her physical beauty makes her attractive to men whereas her "crumpled figure" (65)—a spinal distortion resulting from childbirth—precludes her chances for marriage. Her physical deformity is presented as an impediment to marriage and thus true happiness.

When Sibyl falls in love with St. Clair, Dr. North and his wife worry that she will lose her heart, that her strong romantic nature coupled with her "physical incompleteness" (230) will lead St. Clair to spurn her. Although Sibyl displays a vast amount of knowledge throughout the novel, her intelligence is compromised by her fits of hysterical passion. [31] Her friends Dr. and Mrs. North and Mrs. Vincent overlook her intellect—that she can cite Shakespeare and Goethe—and focus instead on her writing of anonymous poetic love letters to win the love of St. Claire. Alice and Owen North discover these letters, which they regard as dangerous folly because, in their

---

[30] S. Weir Mitchell, *Dr. North and His Friends* (New York: Century, 1900), 18; hereafter cited in the text.

[31] Sibyl Maywood is described as having a dual personality who carries out passionate acts in a somnambulist state.

opinion, St. Claire could never love a deformed person. St. Claire's initial rebuff worsens Sibyl's already unstable emotional condition and weakens her physical condition: she becomes nervous and anemic. Quickly intervening, Dr. North treats Sibyl with the Rest Cure and advises that Sibyl stop writing, rest after every meal, and give up her job as a secretary, because he believes that any type of work is too stressful for her. Exerting his power as a physician, he tells Sibyl that in order to become well again she must not become excited. He treats his patient like a child and exhibits a bedside manner similar to the physician/husband in "The Yellow Wallpaper." Eager to cure herself of nervousness and anemia, Sibyl adheres to all the components of the Rest Cure without hesitation: "I am in bed by your orders, sir, at nine; also, I sleep at once and well" (232). She has confidence in Owen North, obeys her male doctor completely, and is miraculously—and implausibly—cured. Sibyl's physical and emotional ailments virtually disappear as a result of her devotion to the Rest Cure ("the halt in her gait is at times hardly visible" [486]), making her fit for marriage to Victor St. Clair.

Dr. John in "The Yellow Wallpaper" attempts to cure the nameless narrator, as Dr. North did Sibyl, but fails to understand her nature. Not a docile patient like Mitchell's Sibyl or readily susceptible to influence like Alice Leigh, Gilman's protagonist at first subverts Dr. John's treatment by writing secretly. Abandoning her timidity, which Sibyl sustains throughout *Dr. North and His Friends,* the protagonist of "The Yellow Wallpaper" "disagrees" with the diagnosis of the male medical authorities (10). Instead of dutifully climbing into bed after every meal as Sibyl Maywood does, Gilman's narrator escapes what she considers to be punitive rest by feigning sleep. She writes covertly, hiding her journal when she hears John approaching because he "hates to have [her] write a word" (13). If we conceive of the narrator and protagonist as one, she continues to defy John merely through the act of writing her story.[32] Ironically, Gilman's narrator ultimately proves the dangerous consequences of her Rest Cure by remaining entrapped within the sanctity of the home. She actively explores the only text allowed to her—the yellow wallpaper in her prison/sanitarium. Her defiance leads her to crawl in madness in front of Dr. John, who faints before his wife. The nameless narrator of "The Yellow Wallpaper" shows the

---

[32] This issue has recently been raised by Paula Treichler and Richard Feldstein. See Paula A. Treichler, "Escaping the Sentence: Diagnosis and Discourse in 'The Yellow Wallpaper,'" *Tulsa Studies in Women's Literature* 3 (1984): 61–77; Richard Feldstein, "Reader, Text, and Ambiguous Referentiality in 'The Yellow Wallpaper,'" *Feminism and Psychoanalysis,* eds. Richard Feldstein and Judith Roof (Ithaca and London: Cornell University Press, 1989), 269–79.

extreme consequences of living in a society in which the sanctified home proves confining to women. Gilman's narrator illuminates the dangers of following a rigid, restrictive therapeutic treatment. The narrator, though mad, defies the doctor's prescription for healthy eating, moderate exercise, and extended rest and chooses literal madness over John's cure for sanity. In defying her physician's attempt to suppress her, she writes herself into a position of power: she defiantly creeps over John but remains trapped within the home from which Gilman freed herself in order to stay "sane."

Had Gilman's fiction followed Mitchell's prescription for female patients, the righteous Dr. John would not have been "floored"; rather, by following the Rest Cure, the narrator, like Alice Leigh, would have been cured of her ambition to develop her intellect. Gilman concludes that had she herself followed Mitchell's advice, her fate would have been similar to her own narrator's: "It was not a choice between going and staying, but between going, sane, and staying, insane" (*Living*, 97).

In "overwriting" his treatment and the choices available to Mitchell's protagonists, Gilman challenges the happy ending that Mitchell envisions for obedient women. The grimness of Gilman's ending calls attention to the compromises that Mitchell's women make even though they seemingly achieve a happy ending. Although Sibyl Maywood becomes physically cured through following Dr. North's rigid prescription, she does not use her intellectual abilities. In *Dr. North and His Friends* Alice Leigh gains social stature and respectability as Mrs. North, but she loses the very spirit that makes her a compelling female character at the beginning of *Characteristics*.

Rejecting Mitchell's advice—"'And never touch pen, brush or pencil as long as you live'" (96)—Gilman defied Mitchell and the typical behavior he imposed on his female patients both within his medical practice and his fiction. Continuing to revise Mitchell's fictionalization of female patients, she wrote plays, stories, novels, and nonfiction, with *Women and Economics* (1898) bringing her international acclaim. Although she believed that she never fully recovered from the nervous breakdown brought on by the strains of marriage and motherhood, she concluded of her writing: "A brain may lose some faculties and keep others. . . . To write was always as easy to me as to talk. Even my verse, such as it is, flows as smoothly as a letter, is easier in fact" (*Living*, 98–99).[33]

Although only "The Yellow Wallpaper" and *Herland* are well known today, Gilman was as prolific a writer as Mitchell. Like Mitchell's novels, her

---

[33] Gilman mentions in her autobiography that she lost the ability to read for longer than a short period of time. She also had trouble learning languages and following indexes.

own fiction is formulaic, but her stock characters and the formula she prescribes diverge radically from his. Typically, through the intervention of
an older woman, often a doctor, a young and innocent girl breaks from the
restrictions or limitations that endanger her. For example, in "The Girl in
the Pink Hat" (1916) a strong, older woman (whose occupation and name
are never revealed) helps an innocent, courageous girl escape from the
clutches of her criminal boyfriend who has deceived her about his intentions
to marry her.

In "Mr. Peebles' Heart" (1914), Gilman's Dr. Joan Bascom appears to
be the kind of physician Mitchell's Alice Leigh longed to be. In this story
Gilman reverses the typical dynamics of the (male) doctor-(female) patient
relationship. Dr. Bascom's brother-in-law suffers from a nervous breakdown
that results, in her opinion, from his confining occupation, which proves
necessary to support all the women who have clung to him with "tentacles."
Dr. Bascom demands the confidence of her male patient, who protests a bit
but follows her advice as docilely as Mitchell's female patients do Dr. Owen
North. She prescribes a very different cure than S. Weir Mitchell's enforced rest, however—two years of independent travel. Mr. Peebles returns
younger, healthier, stimulated. Without her husband to depend upon during his absence, his wife gains independence. Both improve due to the intervention of Dr. Bascom, who serves as a "new woman" and a role model
for women readers.

Gilman's commitment to advance the lives of women and her understanding of women's problems engage the reader more than the style of her
writing, which sounds hastily crafted at times. Nonetheless, Gilman never
lost her faculty to write: literature offered her an opportunity to challenge
the restrictions imposed upon women. By writing numerous stories voicing
her dedication to improve conditions for women, Gilman defied Mitchell
and the ethos he used to describe women in his fiction. To call upon the apt
title of one of Gilman's own poems, Mitchell became "An Obstacle"[34] both
in real life and fiction, one that Gilman implicated in "The Yellow Wallpaper" and ultimately "overwrote" by touching pen and pencil as long as she
lived.[35]

---

[34] In her foreword to *The Living of Charlotte Perkins Gilman,* Zona Gale includes this poem
along with "Similar Cases" as an indication of Gilman's constant preoccupation with the
advance of women (xxxiii – xxxiv).

[35] This essay grew out of a Collaborative Student-Faculty Research Grant funded by Skid-
more College during the summer of 1990. Erin Senack, now Assistant to the Editor of
Woman of Power magazine, was instrumental in the research involved in this project.

From The Diaries of
Charlotte Perkins Gilman

"Motherhood means———Giving."
March 15, 1885–August 5, 1885

On March 20, 1885, a young nurse, Maria Pease, arrived at the Stetson household to relieve Mrs. Russell, the housekeeper, of her responsibilities. She and Charlotte fast became friends, and Charlotte seemed calmer under her care. They spent the final days before the baby's arrival engaged in long and "delightful" conversations.

Just before 9:00 A.M. on the morning of March 23, 1885, Charlotte gave birth to a daughter, Katharine Beecher Stetson. Her diary comments reporting the birth of her child are sparse but telling:

> Brief ectasy. Long pain.
> Then years of joy again.
>
> Motherhood means———Giving.

The weeks following Katharine's birth were difficult ones, particularly after Maria Pease departed in late April, when her month-long contract was up. For the first time Charlotte was left alone to care for the baby. Her diary entries for May reveal the extent of her anxiety as she tried to cope with the demands of new motherhood. "I wonder what people do who know even less than we about babies! And what women do whose husbands are less— sufficient," she dubiously remarked.

Many years later in her autobiography, Charlotte described in detail the misery she experienced following the birth of Katharine. "I, the ceaselessly industrious, could do no work of any kind. I was so weak that the knife and fork sank from my hands—too tired to eat. I could not read nor write nor paint nor sew nor talk nor listen to talking, nor anything. I lay on that lounge and wept all day. The tears ran down into my ears on either side. I went to bed crying, woke in the night crying, sat on the edge of the bed in the morning and cried—from sheer continuous pain" (*Living*, p. 91). That pain, "a constant dragging weariness" (p. 91), would eventually lead to a nervous breakdown. As the days passed into months, the depression began to consume her.

May 2, the first anniversary of Charlotte and Walter's wedding, was a monumental letdown. "I am tired with long sleeplessness and disappointed at being unable to celebrate the day. So I cry," Charlotte wrote plaintively. Certainly both Charlotte and Walter must have been struck by the difference that a year had made in their relationship. Gone was the thrill of their new-found intimacy. Gone, too, was the innocence of their youthful illusions.

Within a few weeks after Maria Pease's departure, fatigue and depression had taken their toll on Charlotte's nerves. On May 8 she recorded just the latest in a series of adversities: "A fine scare with Miss Baby. She slips off my hand and gets her face under water a moment. Frightens her and me too. Hard day in consequence, she restless and cryful, I tired." The next day Charlotte awoke very tired and depressed. To her utter relief Mary Perkins arrived back from her long trip to Utah in the afternoon. Her return, however, was a mixed blessing.

Charlotte welcomed her mother's help with Katharine, but at the same time the old wounds of never feeling loved by Mary must have resurfaced in full force. The pattern from her own childhood, and the unresolved conflicts, seemed to be mercilessly repeating: "I would hold her close—that lovely child—and instead of love and happiness, feel only pain. The tears ran down on my breast. . . . Nothing was more utterly bitter than this, that even motherhood brought no joy" (*Living*, pp. 91–92).

Mary's apparent ease with the baby also seemed to exacerbate Charlotte's fears of maternal incompetence. "Mother over early," she wrote on May 10. "She takes all the care of the baby day times; washes her today with infinite delight. I fear I shall forget how to take care of the baby." Two days later Charlotte inscribed the date, "Tues. May 12th," but she never wrote the entry that she had apparently intended.

Tuesday, May 12, in fact, marked the beginning of another significant break of nearly three months in Charlotte's diary writing. She attempted again on August 5 to resume her writing, but it wasn't until the end of August that she was able to do so with some regularity. Charlotte had become increasingly depressed during the summer months. Her frustration at not being able to write is evident on August 5 when she lamented that she had "long been ill; weak, nerveless, forced to be idle and let things drift." But as bad as things were, the worst was yet to come.

Sun. March 15th. 1885.

8.30 or 40. Bad night, miserable morning. Weak, draggy, nervous. Lie around. Write some to Mother. Get bed made up with the mattress from upstairs. Mrs. R. does about all the work. Better in the evening. Write note to Mrs. Hazard, and finish mothers letter.

Mon. March 16th. 1885.

7–7.30. Up early on account of Mrs. Sullivan. Partially clean head with fine comb. Get all ready for her. She doesn't come—was to be here at 9—finally arrives to excuse herself and say she'll be here at 1. Attend to my nose, which improves. Julia Jastram calls with little Julia. Brings me some sweet oranges. Kate comes. Julia talks to her till I get faint with the rattle and ask her to stop. Kate stays to dinner. Nice, eat "a much." Then cometh Mrs. S. and I have a nice shampoo. Tires me though. Little nap, broken as usual by Postman. Get up and flourish around abit. Pick up clothes for Belle, etc. Walter. Supper—griddlecakes. Fold hem of napkins and hold forth to Mrs. R. on the Mormon question. Start her to reading "The Fate of Madame La Tour." Walter looks at Rembrandts.

Tues. March. 17th. 1885.

8.35 or so. Bad night with little sleep, but feel pretty well in the morning. Get a nice nap. Mrs. Manchester calls to inquire for me but does not enter. Eat good dinner. Aunt Caroline calls. I read a story in Don Quixote & paint wild rose in Sarah Westcott's album. Walter. Supper. He sketches.

Wed. March 18th. 1885.

8.30 or so. Cold. Feel well. Eat big breakfast. Pick up dishes. Have delicious nap. Mrs. Slicer calls. Dine. Do my usual heavy housework. Sew on necktie for Walter and read in new Harpers. Kate calls. Walter. Supper. Read, Accts.

Thurs. March 19th. 1885.

8.25. Another good day. Nap as usual. Dine. *Wash dishes!* Make another necktie. Read Harpers and Nation. Sing and feel jolly. Louise Diman calls to see how I am. Walter. Supper. Read a little. Write here.

Fri. March 20th. 1885

8.35 or so Up gaily and get good breakfast—chocolate, codfish à la crème, hot biscuit. Get Mrs. Russell over to partake. Eat heartily. Try to sleep afterward but can't, expecting Miss Pease. Blanche W. in about noon. Miss P. at somewhere near 1. Talk much and get dinner. Good. Mrs. R. washes dishes while I show all my things to Miss P. Try to sleep again but can't. Mrs. R.

departs in peace at about 4. Have a real good talk with Miss P. and enjoy it. Like her *very* much. Mrs. Westcott calls. Walter. Supper. Good. She writes. So do I—here.

Sat. March 21st. 1885.

6.30 or so. Belle comes and begins her duties. Does well. Miss Pease continues delightful. Read and talk to her and show her things. Fanny Manchester calls. Miss P. shows her baby things. Afterward I have a nap I'm thankful to say, and feel weak and sleepy again. Belle between two and five, cleaning up etc. Walter, supper, quiet evening. Miss P. gives me my bath. Bed.

Sun. March 22nd. 1885.

7.10 or so. A pleasant day. Enjoy Miss Pease more and more. Sleep some. Read to her. Pale dinner of veal and things. Read some of my things to Miss Pease. Feel weak and sleepy. Write to mother.

March 23rd. 1885.

This day, at about five minuts
to nine in the morning, was born
my child, Katharine.

Brief ectasy. Long pain.
Then years of joy again.

Motherhood means———Giving.

[*After the birth of Katharine, Charlotte neglected her diary for three weeks.*]

Sunday, April 12th. 1885.

First entry in three weeks. Am "up" but not vigorous. Retta Clarke called. Wrote to Mother.

Mon. April 13th. 1885.

Very bright and well, having had good night. Susie and her sister called, bringing me three photos of the children, and one of herself. She was very sweet and nice with the baby. I like her. Miss P. showed pretty baby things to Jennie. Jennie Bucklin called later. Retta came.

Tues. April 14th. 1885.

Still better day, with two or three hour's nap at noon. Mrs. Frank Sheldon & Hattie call. They tire me exceedingly. Retta.

Wed. April 15th. 1885.

Bad night, poor day. Don't sleep much at noon. Blanche W. in. Kate comes. Aunt Caroline. Retta. Kate brought a lovely silver cup for little K., and takes it away to be marked.

Thurs. April 16th. 1885.

Go to ride with Walter—does me *good*. Horrify Miss P. by jumping from the buggy step. Lunch. Nurse baby. Sleep. Get up. Blanche W. in. Dinner, good appetite.

Friday, April 17th. 1885.

Get up while they breakfast. Read and sit around. Two Miss Manchesters call on Miss Pease. I see 'em. Miss P. goes off with them in fine style, to have her photograph taken. Blanche W. comes in and stays with me. I prepare to sleep but the baby wakes. Blanche "changes" her and I nurse her. Then she sleeps again. Belle comes. I dine. Then I have a nice nap and wake lively. Talk to Belle. Miss P. returns with Walter; had a splendid time. Glad she went. Dinner. Nurse baby. Walter draws Miss P. I write rhymes for her sister's knives.

Sat. April 18th. 1885.

Get up and take a bath. Breakfast. Baby for nearly two hours. Then a long nap. Then dinner. Then Baby. Then supper.

[*Another break occurs in the diaries between April 19 and May 1, 1885.*]

May 1885.
Fri. May 1st.

Am pretty well used up by loss of sleep. Walter stays at home in the morning and lets me have a nap. We begin to take ice. Katharine is better; sleeps from 11 till 3, is asleep again before 5 without pain and crying and now remains so at about 7. She has been troubled with indigestion and "wind"; I took some ginger today and think that helped. Mean to leave off cocoa for a while; as we fear it is too rich. She also has a cold. I wonder what people do who know even less than we about babies! And what women do whose husbands are less—sufficient.

Sat. May 2nd. 1885.

The first anniversary of my wedding day. I am tired with long sleeplessness and disappointed at being unable to celebrate the day. So I cry. Walter stays till 12. Belle comes and cleans up for me as usual. I send her for flowers to beautify our little house, and dress myself in black silk, jersey, and yellow crape kerchief. Haven't been "dressed" before in months. Belle is astonished. Walter brings me lovely roses.

Sunday. May 3rd. 1885.

A clear bright lovely day. Go out between 1 & 2, calling on Cousin Mary and Mrs. Diman. Cousin Mary also calls on me; then Mr. & Mrs. Burleigh call, and afterward Guss. Miss Katharine is duly exhibited and behaves well. Get to bed about 9 I think.

Mon. May 4th. 1885.

A good night; baby slept till 3. Get her washed before Walter goes; and after she is asleep proceed to lunch and do housework. Seems good to be at it again. Miss Murphy comes, has a bite, washes part of the dishes, looks over my wardrobe actual and potential, and rehangs my black silk skirt. I tend baby and do a little on bonnet. Telegram from mother. She starts today. O I shall be glad to see her!

Tues. May. 5th. 1885.

Good night again. Good day; baby sleeps well and I sew, write, and dine at ease. Neither does she cry at all, evidently ginger agrees with her via mama. And we gave her chamomille also last night. Lu Manchester calls. Walter, supper, accts, bed.

Wed. May. 6th. 1885.

Katharine developes an unseemly inclination to wake and rise at two o'clock at night or so and remain awake for some hour and a half or two hours. She has a hard day, with considerable cry, very little sleep, and bad "diaper." I am very tired, very. Am starving for fear of giving her the colic. Guess I'd better eat more freely, as she has it anyway.

Thurs. May. 7th. 1885.

Night same as last, only I sleep better while I do sleep. Tired day too; but the baby is well. Eat a banana defiantly with no perceptible ill effect on K. Eat canned peaches; fish (cod) potato, tomato, farina & peaches for dinner. Blanche in.

Fri. May. 8th. 1885.

A fine scare with Miss Baby. She slips off my hand and gets her face under water a moment. Frightens her and me too. Hard day in consequence, she restless and cryful, I tired. Mrs. Westcott comes in at nightfall and revives me much.

Sat. May 9th. 1885.

Another good night—but am very tired and depressed in the morning. Walter shakes me up, sets me to eating, sends me out. I call on Mary and get flowers at Butcher's for mother. Come home with them and then take them up into her room. Home and get things ready to wash baby. At about noon mother comes, bless her, and thereafter all goes well. She worships the baby of course; and to my great relief and joy declares her perfectly well. We have a happy afternoon. Mary Chafee calls. Walter comes, but goes out again after dinner to post letters and get some old rum for mother, who has a heavy cold. I go over to her room with her.

Sun. May. 10th. 1885.

Not very good night. Mother over early. She takes all the care of the baby day times; washes her today with infinite delight. I fear I shall forget how to take care of the baby. Alice comes to see Aunt Mary in the morning; and later with her mother. Jennie and her husband call. I get dinner, and Walter and I go to walk afterward. Mother goes to bed early. Mrs. Westcott calls.

Mon. May. 11th. 1885.

Fair night's sleep. Good day. So nice to have mother here. I wash dishes again. Anna comes, would have been surprised but for Mary. She brings

Clarence in the evening, and he *is* surprised. Another blanket comes—from Miss Alden.

Tuesday (August) 4th.

[*Charlotte apparently intended to write an entry but did not.*]

August. 5th. 1885———

5.30 Yesterday I arranged my books once more; hoping to be able to keep account of my life and expenses again. I have long been ill; weak, nerveless, forced to be idle and let things drift. Perhaps now I can pick up the broken threads again and make out some kind of a career after all. Arose this morning at 5.30 and nursed the baby. Took my Mellin's Food as usual and got breakfast. Mine consisted of cocoa and a little bread. Nurse again at 8.45. Then write.

Sample Student Research Paper

Justino 1

Erin Justino
Professor Daniels
English 102
14 October 1997

Concepts of Confinement and Escape in
Charlotte Perkins Gilman's "The Yellow Wallpaper"

The central concern of the main character in
Charlotte Perkins Gilman's "The Yellow Wallpaper"
is where and how she and her husband will spend
the summer. Their summer house is described four
times in the first two sentences of the story,
but it is the last descriptive phrase, "a haunted
house," that offers the first foreshadowing of
the themes and events in this story ("Yellow
Wallpaper" 13). Why does Jane choose the word
<u>haunted</u> to describe the house? Why does she ex-
press concern at all? As we seek answers to these
questions and go on to discover the room with
the yellow wallpaper, we learn more about Jane's
confinement or imprisonment, not only in the
house but also in her relationship with her husband John, and with society. At the end of the
story, we see that despite Jane's efforts to escape her confinements, any escape is only temporary. Even her final escape into madness poses
as much of a problem as a solution.

Jane senses immediately that something about
the summer house does not feel comfortable to
her: "There is something queer about it" (13).

Introduction

Thesis statement

First possible reason for Jane's sense of confinement: not being heard

Before she can express her feelings and be
heard, she tells us how her husband laughs at
her, thereby devaluing and even erasing her ideas.
After all, John is an esteemed professional, a
doctor (as is Jane's brother), and their appraisal
of Jane's condition and of the house must therefore be authoritative (Golden 96).

Unfortunately, Jane is unable to challenge
John directly; he makes all the decisions in
their marriage. Jane wrestles with internal conflict. She feels ungrateful because she knows she
does not express appreciation for her "special
treatment," but when she finds the treatment disagreeable, she feels "unreasonably angry" (14).
Trapped by the gap between what she experiences
and what she is allowed to express, Jane is exhausted throughout much of this story; the effort
required to cope with these conflicts depletes
her energy, day by day.

> Discussion of failure to escape from confinement

When John selects the upstairs nursery for
her convalescence, Jane registers the oddities of
the room: barred windows, "rings and things in
the walls," and a wallpaper that "commits every
artistic sin" (15). Forbidden from writing in
her journal, Jane turns to the only paper available to her, the wallpaper that has been partially stripped by the former occupants. The
extent of her dislike for the wallpaper should
serve as a warning that Jane is not responding
well to her treatment, but John does not pick up
on this clue (Gilbert and Gubar 34). Slowly but

> Second possible reason for Jane's sense of confinement: actual physical confinement

Justino 3

surely, Jane begins to seek comfort and escape in
the only paper available to her (Romain).

At one point Jane almost regains some sense
of reality. She recognizes that her condition involves depression and that she seems not able
to do the things she wants to do. She understands
that even her child, "a dear baby," upsets her,
and she is grateful for the help of Mary, the
child's nurse. She proposes to redecorate her
room, to replace the hideous wallpaper, but John
convinces her they are only there for the summer,
that he does not wish to become involved in any
extended renovation, and he calls her "a blessed
little goose" (16). Unable, once again, to make
her feelings understandable to John, Jane turns
her gaze outward, and we see the transition
from her acceptance of confinement to her real-
ization of the need to escape. Outside her window, Jane sees things "mysterious," "riotous,"
"knarly" (16), and when she finally looks back
on her room, she knows she must take action
against the "vicious influence" that confines
her (16).

By the Fourth of July, John senses that Jane
is not improving as he had anticipated. He announces that she may have to be sent to the famous neurologist Dr. Silas Weir Mitchell for
treatment. Jane knows of Mitchell and his treatment and wants no part of this plan (Golden
96). She cries and sinks further into depression, withdrawing still further from reality. The

Jane's need to escape

Jane's transition into madness

Justino 4

paper in her room preoccupies her, and she discovers all sorts of grotesque patterns and feelings in it. It has become symbolic of all that
confines her, and yet she is determined to over-
come her situation. Growing bold, Jane begins
stripping the paper off the walls, searching for
the lost woman she imagines is hiding behind it:
"I pulled and she shook, I shook and she pulled,
and before morning we had pulled off yards of
that paper" (26). As she continues her work Jane
is transformed into the trapped woman, and liberation of a sort seems close at hand.

When John knocks at Jane's door on the day
they are to leave the house, Jane refuses to let
him in. The Jane he knew has become trapped in
the wallpaper, escaped in a way no one anticipated. When John finally breaks into the room, he
discovers a creature crawling on her hands and
knees who tells him, "I've got out at last"
(27), and he promptly faints. The Jane/creature
does not bolt from the room but continues to
creep "over him every time" (27) she circles the
room. She has fashioned the only "escape" available to her. But even this escape creates problems for Jane, for what will happen to her when
John awakens?

After the birth of her daughter, Charlotte
Perkins Gilman suffered just as Jane did in "The
Yellow Wallpaper." Gilman underwent the Mitchell
Rest Cure and nearly went insane. She recovered
only when she decided to make her own life, free

Jane's escape

Conclusion

from husband, family, and social constraints.
She tells us that she wrote "The Yellow Wallpaper" to spare others the trauma she suffered
and to make Mitchell and all doctors aware of
the damage they had done (Gilman, "Why" 33).
In addition, she created a stunning work of literature that describes the conditions under which
many women lived during the nineteenth century,
and that presents a powerful view of the effects
of social and physical confinement--and the dangers of limited escape.

Justino 6

Works Cited

Gilbert, Sandra M., and Susan Gubar. <u>The Madwoman
in the Attic: The Woman Writer and the Nineteenth Century Literary Imagination</u>. New
Haven: Yale UP, 1979. Kivo 44-46.

Gilman, Charlotte Perkins. "The Yellow Wallpaper." Kivo 23-35.

---. "Why I Wrote 'The Yellow Wallpaper.'" <u>Fore-
runner</u> 4 (1913): 271. Kivo 40-41.

Golden, Catherine. "'Overwriting' the Rest Cure:
Charlotte Perkins Gilman's Literary Escape
from S. Weir Mitchell's Fictionalization of
Women." <u>Critical Essays on Charlotte Perkins
Gilman</u>. Ed. Joanne B. Kaysinski. New York:
Hall, 1992. Kivo 83-90.

Kivo, Carol, ed. <u>The Harcourt Brace Casebook Series in Literature: "The Yellow Wallpaper"</u>.
Fort Worth: Harcourt, 1997.

Bibliography

Works by Charlotte Perkins Gilman

FICTION

Gilman, Charlotte Perkins. *The Charlotte Perkins Gilman Reader.* Edited with introduction by Ann J. Lane. New York: Pantheon, 1980.

———. *Benigna Machiavelli.* Not published: Bandana, 1994.

———. *The Crux.* New York: Charlton, 1911.

———. *Herland.* With introduction by Ann J. Lane. New York: Pantheon, 1979.

———. *Moving the Mountain.* New York: Charlton, 1911.

———. *Unpunished.* Eds. Catherine J. Golden and Denise D. Knight. New York: Feminist, 1997.

———. *What Diantha Did.* New York: Charlton, 1910; London: Fisher, 1912.

———. "The Yellow Wallpaper." *New England Magazine* 5 (January 1892): 647–46.

———. *The Yellow Wallpaper.* Boston: Small, 1899. Reprint, with an afterword by Elaine Hedges. Old Westbury, NY: Feminist, 1973.

NONFICTION

Gilman, Charlotte Perkins. *Concerning Children.* Boston: Small, 1900, 1901; London: Putnam's, 1900.

———. *The Diaries of Charlotte Perkins Gilman.* Ed. Denise D. Knight. Charlottesville: U of Virginia P, 1994.

———. *His Religion and Hers: A Study of the Faith of Our Fathers and the Work of Our Mothers.* New York and London: Century, 1923; London: Fisher, 1924. Reprint. Westport, CT.: Hyperion, 1976.

———. *The Home: Its Work and Influence.* New York: McClure, 1903; London: Heinemann, 1904. Reprint. New York: Source, 1970.

———. *Human Work.* New York: McClure, 1904.

———. *A Journey From Within: The Love Letters of Charlotte Perkins Gilman, 1897–1900.* Ed. Mary A. Hill. Lewisburg, PA: Bucknell UP; London: Associated UP, 1995.

———. *The Labor Movement.* Paper read before the trade and labor unions of

Alameda County, CA, 2 Sep. 1892. Oakland, CA: Alameda County Federation of Trades, 1893.

————. *The Living of Charlotte Perkins Gilman: An Autobiography.* New York and London: Appleton–Century, 1935. Reprint. New York: Arno P, 1972; Harper, 1975.

————. *The Man-Made World; or, Our Androcentric Culture.* New York: Charlton, 1911. Reprint. New York: Source, 1970.

————. *Women and Economics: A Study of the Economic Relation Between Men and Women as a Factor in Social Evolution.* Boston: Small, 1898. Reprint, edited with introduction by Carl N. Degler. New York: Harper, 1966; Source, 1970.

VERSE

Gilman, Charlotte Perkins. *In This Our World.* Oakland, CA: McCombs, 1893; London: Fisher, 1895. 2nd ed. San Francisco: James H. Barry, 1895.

————. *Suffrage Songs and Verses.* New York: Charlton, 1911.

Works about
Charlotte Perkins Gilman

BIBLIOGRAPHY

Scharnhorst, Gary. *Charlotte Perkins Gilman: A Bibliography.* New York: Scarecrow, 1985.

BIOGRAPHY

Berkin, Carol. "Private Woman, Public Woman: The Contradictions of Charlotte Perkins Gilman." *Women in America: A History.* Ed. Ruth Berkin and Mary Beth Norton. Boston: Houghton, 1979. 150–73.

Cooper, James L., and Sheila McIsaac Cooper. *The Roots of American Feminist Thought.* Boston: Allyn, 1973. 177–92.

Gale, Zona. Foreword. *The Living of Charlotte Perkins Gilman.* New York and London: Appleton-Century, 1935. xiii–xxxviii.

Hill, Mary A. *Charlotte Perkins Gilman: The Making of a Radical Feminist 1860–1885.* Philadelphia: Temple UP, 1980.

Lane, Ann J. *To Herland and Beyond: The Life and Work of Charlotte Perkins Gilman.* New York: Pantheon, 1990.

Myerling, Sheryle L., Ed. *Charlotte Perkins Gilman: The Woman and Her Work.* Ann Arbor: UMI Research, 1989.

Nies, Judith. *Seven Women.* New York: Viking, 1977.

Pringle, Mary Beth. "Charlotte Perkins Stetson Gilman." *American Women Writers.* New York: Ungar, 1980.

Winkler, Barbara Scott. *Victorian Daughters: The Lives and Feminism of Charlotte Perkins Gilman and Olive Schreimer.* Michigan Occasional Paper No. 13. Ann Arbor: U of Michigan P, 1980.

CRITICISM AND COMMENTARY

Allen, Polly Wynn. *Building Domestic Liberty: Charlotte Perkins Gilman's Architectural Feminism.* Amherst: U of Massachusetts P, 1988.

Bader, Julia. "The Dissolving Vision: Realism in Jewett, Freeman and Gilman." *American Realism: New Essays.* Ed. Eric J. Sundquist. Baltimore: Johns Hopkins UP, 1982. 176–98.

Bair, Barbara. "Double Discourse: Gilman, Sarton, and the Subversive Text." *That Great Sanity: Critical Essays on May Sarton.* Ed. Susan Swartzlander, et al. Ann Arbor: U of Michigan P, 1992. 187–208.

Bak, John S. "Escaping the Jaundiced Eye: Foucaldian Panopticism in Charlotte Perkins Gilman's 'The Yellow Wallpaper.'" *Studies in Short Fiction* 31.1 (1994): 39–46.

Biamonte, Gloria A. "'. . . There Is A Story, If We Could Only Find It': Charlotte Perkins Gilman's 'The Giant Wisteria.'" *Legacy* 5.2 (1988): 33–43.

Bleich, David. "Sexism and the Discourse of Perfection." *American Transcendental Quarterly* 3.1 (1989): 11–25.

Boa, Elizabeth. "Creepy-Crawlies: Gilman's 'The Yellow Wallpaper' and Kafka's *The Metamorphosis.*" *Paragraph* 13.1 (1990): 19–29.

Boyles, Mary. "Woman: The Inside Outsider." *Selected Essays from the International Conference on The Outsider 1988.* Ed. John M. Crafton. Carrollton: W. Georgia College, 1990. 117–25.

Brown, Gillian. "The Empire of Agrophobia." *Representations* 20 (Fall 1987): 134–57.

Burton, Deidre. "Linguistic Innovation in Feminist Utopian Fiction." *Ilha do Desterro* 14.2 (1985): 82–106.

Cane, Aleta. "Charlotte Perkins Gilman's *Herland* as a Feminist Response to Male Quest Romance." *Jack London Journal* 2 (1995): 25–38.

Crew, Jonathan. "Queering 'The Yellow Wallpaper': Charlotte Perkins Gilman and the Politics of Form." *Tulsa Studies in Women's Literature.* 14.2 (1995): 273–87.

Crocco, Margaret S. "Women's History in the 1920s: A Look at Anzia Yezierska and Charlotte Perkins Gilman." *Social Education* 59.1 (1995): 29–31.

Davidson, Cathy N. *Charlotte Perkins Gilman: The Woman and Her Work.* Ann Arbor, Michigan UMI Research, 1989.

Deitz, Frank. "Women's Space: The Fiction of Charlotte Perkins Gilman." *Indian Journal of American Studies* 19.1–2 (1989): 19–27.

DeLamotte, Eugenia C. "Male and Female Mysteries in 'The Yellow Wallpaper.'" *Legacy* 5.1 (1988): 3–14.

Delashmit, Margaret and Charles Long. "Gilman's 'The Yellow Wallpaper.'" *Explicator* 5.1 (1991): 32–33.

Dimmock, Wai Chee. "Feminism, New Historicism, and the Reader." *Readers in History: Nineteenth Century American Literature and the Contexts of Response.* Ed. James Machor. Baltimore: Hopkins UP, 1993. 85–106.

Dock, Julie Bates. "'But One Expects That': Charlotte Perkins Gilman's 'The Yellow Wallpaper' and the Shifting Light of Scholarship." *PMLA* 8, n 1 (1996): 52–66.

Donaldson, Laura E. "The Eve of De-Struction: Charlotte Perkins Gilman and the Feminist Recreation of Paradise." *Women's Studies* 16 (1989): 373–87.

Doyle, William T. *Charlotte Perkins Gilman and the Cycle of Feminist Reform.* N.p., 1960.

Feldstein, Richard, and Judith Roof, eds. *Feminism and Psychoanalysis.* Ithaca: Cornell UP, 1989. 255–79.

Fetterly, Judith. "Reading About Reading: 'A Jury of Her Peers,' 'The Murders in the Rue Morgue,' and 'The Yellow Wallpaper.'" *Gender and Reading: Essays on Readers, Texts, and Contexts.* Ed. Elizabeth Flynn, et al. Baltimore: Johns Hopkins UP, 1986. 147–64.

Fleenor, Julian E., ed. *The Female Gothic.* Montreal: Eden, 1983. 227–41.

Freibert, Lucy M. "World Views in Utopian Novels by Women." *Women and Utopia.* Ed. Marleen Barr, et al. Maryland: UP of America, 1983. 67–84.

Friedman, Susan S. "Women's Autobiographical Selves: Theory and Practice." *The Private Self: Theory and Practice of Women's Autobiographical Writings.* Ed. Shari Benstock. Chapel Hill: U of North Carolina P, 1988. 34–62.

Fryer, Judith. "Women and Space: The Flowering of Desire." *Prospects* 9 (1984): 187–230.

Gleason, William. "'Find Their Place and Fall in Line': The Revisioning of Women's Work in *Herland* and 'Emma McChesney & Co.'s'." *Prospects* 21 (1996): 39–88.

Golden, Catherine. "'Light of the Home, Light of the World': The Presentation of Motherhood in Gilman's Short Fiction." *Modern Language Studies* 26.2–3 (1996): 135–47.

———. "The Writing of 'The Yellow Wallpaper': A Double Palimpsest." *Studies in American Fiction* 17.2 (1989): 193–201.

Golden, Catherine, ed. *The Captive Imagination: a Casebook on 'The Yellow Wallpaper'.* New York: Feminist, 1992.

Gordon, Rae B. "Interior Decoration in Poe and Gilman." *Literature Interpretation Theory* 3.2 (1991): 85–99.

Gormick, Vivian. "Twice Told Tales." *Nation,* 23 Sep. 1978, 278–81.

Gough, Val. "Lesbians and Virgins: The Motherland in *Herland.*" *Anticipations:*

Essays on Early Science Fiction and Its Precursors. Ed. David Seed. New York: Syracuse UP, 1995. 195–215.

Graulich, Melody. "'I Thought At First She Was Talking About Herself': Mary Austin on Charlotte Perkins Gilman." *Jack London Journal* 1 (1994): 148–58.

Gubar, Susan. "She and *Herland:* Feminism as Fantasy." *Coordinates: Placing Science Fiction and Fantasy.* Ed. George Slusser, et al. Carbondale: S. Illinois P, 1983. 139–49.

Hadas, Pamela W. "Madness and Medicine: The Graphomaniac's Cure." *Literature and Medicine* 9 (1990): 181–93.

Haney-Peritz, Janice. "Monumental Feminism and Literature's Ancestral House: Another Look at 'The Yellow Wallpaper.'" *Women's Studies* 12.2 (1986): 113–28.

Hayden, Dolores. "Charlotte Perkins Gilman and the Kitchenless House." *S.L.: Radical History Review.* 1979.

Hedges, Elaine R. Afterword. *The Yellow Wallpaper.* Old Westbury, NY: Feminist, 1973, 37–63.

Heller, Scott. "How A Writer Became A Feminist Legend." *The Chronicle of Higher Education* 42.19 (1996): A10.

Herndl, Diane P. "The Writing Cure: Charlotte Perkins Gilman, Anna O., and 'Hysterical Writing.'" *NSWA-Journal* 1.1 (1988): 52–74.

Hill, Mary A. "Charlotte Perkins Gilman: A Feminist's Struggle with Womanhood." *Massachusetts Review* 21.3 (1980): 503–26.

Hong, Sung-joo. "Charlotte Perkins Gilman's 'The Yellow Wallpaper': The Wallpaper as a Split Self and a Disruptive Text." *The Journal of English Language and Literature* 41.3 (1995): 697–719.

Huckle, Patricia. "Women in Utopias." *The Utopian Vision: Seven Essays on the Quincentennial of Sir Thomas More.* Ed. E.D.S. Sullivan. San Diego: San Diego State UP, 1983. 115–36.

Hume, Beverly A. "Gilman's 'Interminable Grotesque': the Narrator of 'The Yellow Wallpaper.'" *Studies in Short Fiction.* 28.4 (1991): 477–85.

Johnston, Georgia. "Exploring Lack and Absence in the Body/Text: Charlotte Perkins Gilman Prewriting Irigaray." *Women's Studies.* 21.1 (1992): 75–86.

——. "Three Men in *Herland:* Why They Enter the Text." *Utopian Studies IV.* Ed. Ouvrard Leibacher and Nicholas Smith. Maryland: UP of America, 1990. 55–59.

Johnson, Greg. "Gilman's Gothic Allegory: Rage and Redemption in 'The Yellow Wallpaper.'" *Studies in Short Fiction.* 26.4 (1989): 521–31.

Jones, Libby F., ed., et al. *Feminism, Utopia, and Narrative.* Knoxville: U of Tennessee P, 1990. 100–29.

Kasmer, Lisa. "Charlotte Perkins Gilman's 'The Yellow Wallpaper': A Symptomatic Reading." *Literature and Psychology.* 36.3 (1990): 1–16.

Karpinski, Joanne B., ed. *Critical Essays on Charlotte Perkins Gilman.* New York: Hall; Toronto: Maxwell, 1992.

Kautz, Elizabeth D. "Gynecologists, Power and Sexuality in Modernist Texts." *Journal of Popular Culture* 28.4 (1995): 81–91.

Kennard, Jean E. "Convention Coverage or How to Read Your Own Life." *New Literary History* 8.1 (1981): 69–88.

Kessler, Carol F. "Brittle Jars and Bitter Jangles: Light Verse by Charlotte Perkins Gilman." *Regionalism and the Female Imagination* 4.2 (1978): 35–43.

———. *Charlotte Perkins Gilman: Her Progress Toward Utopia with Selected Writings.* New York: Syracuse UP, 1995.

———. "Consider Her Ways: The Cultural Work of Charlotte Perkins Gilman's Pragmatopian Stories, 1908–1913." *Utopian and Science Fiction by Women: Worlds of Difference.* Ed. Jane Donawerth and Carol Kolmerten. Syracuse: Syracuse UP, 1994. 126–36.

Keyser, Elizabeth. "Looking Backward from *Herland* to *Gulliver's Travels.*" *Studies in American Fiction* 11.1 (1983): 31–46.

King, Jeannette, and Pam Morris. "On Not Reading Between the Lines: Models of Reading in 'The Yellow Wallpaper.'" *Studies in Short Fiction.* 26.1 (1989): 23–33.

Knight, Denise D. "Charlotte Perkins Gilman's Forgotten First Publication." *ANQ* 7.4 (1994): 223–25.

———. Knight, Denise D., ed. *'The Yellow Wallpaper' and Selected Stories of Charlotte Perkins Gilman.* New York: U of Delaware P, 1994.

———. "'With the First Blade of Grass': Whitman's Influence on the Poetry of Charlotte Perkins Gilman." *Walt Whitman Quarterly Review* 11.1 (1993): 18–29.

———. *Charlotte Perkins Gilman: A Study of the Short Fiction.* New York: Twayne; London: Prentice, 1997.

———. "The Reincarnation of Jane: 'Through This'—Gilman's Companion to 'The Yellow Wallpaper.'" *Women's Studies.* 20.3–3 (1992): 287–302.

Kolodny, Annette. "A Map for Rereading: or Gender and the Interpretation of Literary Texts." *New Literary History,* 11 (Spring 1980): 455–60.

Krieg, Joann P. "Charlotte Perkins Gilman and the Whitman Connection." *Walt Whitman Review* 1.4 (1984): 21–25.

Lancaster, Jane. "'I Could Easily Have Been an Acrobat': Charlotte Perkins Gilman and the Providence Ladies' Sanitary Gymnasium 1881–1884." *American Transcendental Quarterly* 8.1 (1994): 33–52.

Lane, Ann J. Introduction. *Herland* by Charlotte Perkins Gilman. New York: Pantheon, 1979.

———. "The Fictional World of Charlotte Perkins Gilman." Introduction. *The Charlotte Perkins Gilman Reader.* New York: Pantheon, 1980. ix–xlii.

Lanser, Susan S. "Feminist Criticism, 'The Yellow Wallpaper,' and the Politics of Color in America." *Feminist Studies.* 15.3 (1989): 415–43.

MacPike, Loralee. "Environment as Psychopathological Symbolism in 'The Yellow Wallpaper.'" *American Literary Realism,* 8 (Summer, 1975), 286–88.

Magner, Lois N. "Women and the Scientific Idiom: Textual Episodes from Woll-stonecraft, Fuller, and Firestone." *Signs* 4 (1978): 61–80.

Makowsky, Veronica. "Fear of Feeling and the Turn-of-the-Century Woman of Letters." *American Literary History* 5.2 (1993): 326–34.

Masse, Michelle A. "Gothic Repetition: Husbands, Horrors, and Things That Go Bump in the Night." *Signs.* 15.4 (1990): 679–713.

Matossian, Lou Ann. "A Woman-Made Language: Charlotte Perkins Gilman and *Herland.*" *Women and Language* 10.2 (1987): 16–20.

Miller, Margaret. "The Ideal Woman in Two Feminist Science-Fiction Utopias." *Science Fiction Studies* 10.2 (1983): 191–98.

Owens, Suzanne E. "The Ghostly Double Behind the Wallpaper in Charlotte Perkins Gilman's 'The Yellow Wallpaper.'" *Haunting the House of Fiction: Feminist Perspectives on Ghost Stories by American Women.* Ed. Lynette Carpenter and Wendy Kolmar. Knoxville: U of Tennessee P, 1991. 64–79.

Pearson, Carol. "Coming Home: Four Feminist Utopias and Patriarchal Experience." *Future Females: A Critical Anthology* Ed. Marleen Barr. Bowling Green: Bowling Green State U Poplar P, 1981. 63–70.

Peysor, Thomas G. "Reproducing Utopia: Charlotte Perkins and *Herland.*" *Studies in American Fiction* 20.1 (1992): 1–16.

Poiror, Suzanne. "The Weir Mitchell Rest Cure: Doctor and Patients." *Women's Studies* 10.1 (1983): 15–40.

Post, Stephen L. "His and Hers: Mental Breakdown as Depicted by Evelyn Waugh and Charlotte Perkins Gilman." *Literature and Medicine* 9 (1990): 172–80.

Pringle, Mary Beth. "La Poetique de l'esace' in Charlotte Perkins Gilman's 'The Yellow Wallpaper.'" *The French American Review* 3 (1979): 15–22.

Rawls, Melanie. "*Herland* and Out of the Silent Planet." *Mythlore* 13.2 (1986): 51–54.

Robinson, Lillian S. "Killing Patriarchy: Charlotte Perkins Gilman, the Murder Mystery, and Post-Feminist Propaganda." *Tulsa Studies in Women's Literature* 10.2 (1991): 273–85.

———. "Charlotte Perkins Gillman's 'The Giant Wisteria': A Hieroglyph of the Female Frontier Gothic." *Frontier Gothic: Terror and Wonder at the Frontier in American Literature.* Ed. David Mogen, et al. New Jersey: Dickinson UP, 1993. 156–74.

———. "Making Her Fame: Charlotte Perkins Gilman in California." *California History* 64.3 (1985): 192–201.

Rose, Jane Atteridge. "Images of Self: The Example of Rebecca Harding Davis and Charlotte Perkins Gilman." *English Language Notes.* 29.4 (1992): 70–78.

Schöpp-Schilling, Beate. "'The Yellow Wallpaper': A Rediscovered 'Realistic' Story." *American Literary Realism,* 8 (Summer, 1975), 284–86.

Seigfried, Charlene H. "Classical American Philosophy's Invisible Women." *Canadian Review of American Studies* (1992): 83–116.

Shumaker, Conrad. "Realism, Reform, and the Audience: Charlotte Perkins Gilman's Unreadable Wallpaper." *Arizona Quarterly* 47.1 (1991): 81–93.

———. "'Too Terribly Good To Be Printed': Charlotte Perkins Gilman's 'The Yellow Wallpaper.'" *American Literature* 57.4 (1985): 588–99.

Smith, Margaret J. "Charlotte Perkins Gilman and Emma Goldman, Reformer and Radical." *Arkansas Review* 3.2 (1994): 152–67.

Smith, Marsha A. "The Disoriented Male Narrator and Societal Conversion: Charlotte Perkins Gilman's Feminist Utopian Vision." *American Transcendental Quarterly* 3.1 (1989): 123–33.

"The Woman of To-Day and of To-Morrow: Woman's Economic Place: To Reply to the Article of Professor Peck's in the June Cosmopolitan." *Jack London Journal* 1 (1994): 109–47.

Treichler, Paula A. "Escaping the Sentence: Diagnosis and Discourse in 'The Yellow Wallpaper.'" *Tulsa Studies in Women's Literature* 3.1–2 (1984): 61–77.

Veeder, William. "Who Is Jane? The Intricate Feminism of Charlotte Perkins Gilman." *Arizona Quarterly* 44.3 (1988): 40–79.

Weinstein, Lee. "'The Yellow Wallpaper': A Supernatural Interpretation." *Studies in Weird Fiction* 4 (Fall, 1988): 23–35.

Wiessenthal, C.W. "'Unheard-of Contradictions': The Language of Madness in C.P. Gilman's 'The Yellow Wallpaper.'" *Wascana Review* 25.2 (1990): 1–17.

Will, Barbara. "Nervous Systems, 1880–1915." *American Bodies: Cultural Histories of the Physique.* Ed. Tim Armstrong. New York: New York UP, 1996. 86–100.

Wilson, Christopher P. "Charlotte Perkins Gilman's Steady Burghers: The Terrain of *Herland.*" *Women's Studies* 12.3 (1986): 271–92.

ELECTRONIC AND MEDIA SOURCES

Film and Video
The Yellow Wallpaper. Writ. and Dir. Tony Romain. Prod. Margaret Lucas. Vision Films, 1996.

SOUND RECORDINGS

Agnes Moorhead, reader. *The Yellow Wallpaper.* CBS. Audiocassette, 1980.

Claudette Sutherland, reader. *The Yellow Wallpaper.* Spencer Library. Audiocassette, n.d.

WORLD WIDE WEB SITES

American Literature Discussion Group. Professor Daniel Anderson. U of Texas. Spring 1997 <http://www.en.cwrl.utexas.edu/˜daniel/amlit/wallpaper/wallpaper.html>.

Charlotte Perkins Gilman Newsletter. Ed. Denise Knight. 1995, 96, 97. SUNY Cortland. May 1997 <http://www.orchard.cortland.edu/gilmanNews/gilmanNews95.html>.

Women's History. Professor Lavender. City University of New York. Spring 1997 <http:www.Library.csi.cuny.edu/dept/history/lavender/ywdiscuss.html>.

Women's Studies. Professor Joan Korenman. U of Maryland. May 1997 <http://www.umbc.edu/˜korenman/wmst/simplesearch.html>.

Appendix:
Documenting Sources

A Guide to MLA
Documentation Style

Documentation is the acknowledgment of information from an outside source that you use in a paper. In general, you should give credit to your sources whenever you quote, paraphrase, summarize, or in any other way incorporate borrowed information or ideas into your work. Not to do so—on purpose or by accident—is to commit **plagiarism,** to appropriate the intellectual property of others. By following accepted conventions of documentation, you not only help avoid plagiarism, but also show your readers that you write with care and precision. In addition, you enable them to distinguish your ideas from those of your sources and, if they wish, to locate and consult the sources you cite.

Not all ideas from your sources need to be documented. You can assume that certain information—facts from encyclopedias, textbooks, newspapers, magazines, and dictionaries, or even from television and radio—is common knowledge. Even if the information is new to you, it need not be documented as long as it is found in several reference sources and as long as you do not use the exact wording of your source. Information that is in dispute or that is the original contribution of a particular person, however, *must* be documented. You need not, for example, document the fact that Arthur Miller's *Death of a Salesman* was first performed in 1949 or that it won a Pulitzer Prize for drama. (You could find this information in any current encyclopedia.) You would, however, have to document a critic's interpretation of a performance or a scholar's analysis of an early draft of the play, even if you do not use your source's exact words.

Students of literature use the documentation style recommended by the Modern Language Association of America (MLA), a professional organization of more than twenty-five thousand teachers and students of English and other languages. This method of documentation, the one that you should use any time you write a literature paper, has three components: *parenthetical references in the text, a list of works cited,* and *explanatory notes.*

Parenthetical References in the Text

MLA documentation uses references inserted in parentheses within the text that refer to an alphabetical list of works cited at the end of the paper. A typical **parenthetical reference** consists of the author's last name and a page number.

> Gwendolyn Brooks uses the sonnet form to create poems that have a wide social and aesthetic range (Williams 972).

If you use more than one source by the same author, include a shortened title in the parenthetical reference. In the following entry, "Brooks's Way" is a shortened form of the complete title of the article "Gwendolyn Brooks's Way with the Sonnet."

> Brooks not only knows Shakespeare, Spenser, and Milton, but she also knows the full range of African-American poetry (Williams, "Brooks's Way" 972).

If you mention the author's name or the title of the work in your paper, only a page reference is necessary.

> According to Gladys Margaret Williams in "Gwendolyn Brooks's Way with the Sonnet," Brooks combines a sensitivity to poetic forms with a depth of emotion appropriate for her subject matter (972-73).

Keep in mind that you use different punctuation for parenthetical references used with *paraphrases and summaries*, with *direct quotations run in with the text*, and with *quotations of more than four lines*.

Paraphrases and Summaries

Place the parenthetical reference after the last word of the sentence and before the final punctuation:

> In her works Brooks combines the pessimism of Modernist poetry with the optimism of the Harlem Renaissance (Smith 978).

Direct quotations run in with the text

Place the parenthetical reference after the quotation marks and before the final punctuation:

> According to Gary Smith, Brooks's <u>A Street in Bronzeville</u> "conveys the primacy of suffering in the lives of poor Black women" (980).

> According to Gary Smith, the poems in <u>A Street in Bronzeville</u>, "served notice that Brooks had learned her craft . . ." (978).

> Along with Thompson we must ask, "Why did it take so long for critics to acknowledge that Gwendolyn Brooks is an important voice in twentieth-century American poetry?" (123)

Quotations set off from the text

Omit the quotation marks and place the parenthetical reference one space after the final punctuation.

> For Gary Smith, the identity of Brooks's African-American women is inextricably linked with their sense of race and poverty:
>
>> For Brooks, unlike the Renaissance poets, the victimization of poor Black women becomes not simply a minor chord but a predominant theme of <u>A Street in Bronzeville</u>. Few, if any, of her female characters are able to free themselves from a web of poverty that threatens to strangle their lives. (980)

[Quotations of more than four lines are indented ten spaces (or one inch) from the margin and are not enclosed within quotation marks. The first line of a single paragraph of quoted material is not indented further. If you quote two or more paragraphs, indent the first line of each paragraph three additional spaces (one-quarter inch).]

SAMPLE REFERENCES

The following formats are used for parenthetical references to various kinds of sources used in papers about literature. (Keep in mind that the parenthetical reference contains just enough information to enable readers to find the source in the list of works cited at the end of the paper.)

An entire work

    August Wilson's play Fences treats many themes fre-
    quently expressed in modern drama.

[When citing an entire work, state the name of the author in your paper instead of in a parenthetical reference.]

A work by two or three authors

    Myths cut across boundaries and cultural spheres and
    reappear in strikingly similar forms from country to
    country (Feldman and Richardson 124).

    The effect of a work of literature depends on the
    audience's predispositions that derive from member-
    ship in various social groups (Hovland, Janis, and
    Kelley 87).

A work by more than three authors

    Hawthorne's short stories frequently use a combi-
    nation of allegorical and symbolic methods (Guerin
    et al. 91).

[The abbreviation *et al.* is Latin for "and others."]

A work in an anthology

    In his essay "Flat and Round Characters" E. M. For-
    ster distinguishes between one-dimensional charac-
    ters and those that are well developed (Stevick
    223-31).

[The parenthetical reference cites the anthology (edited by Stevick) that contains Forster's essay; full information about the anthology appears in the list of works cited.]

A work with volume and page numbers

In 1961 one of Albee's plays, <u>The Zoo Story</u>, was
finally performed in America (Eagleton 2:17).

An indirect source

Wagner observed that myth and history stood before
him "with opposing claims" (qtd. in Winkler 10).

[The abbreviation *qtd. in* (quoted in) indicates that the quoted material was
not taken from the original source.]

A play or poem with numbered lines

"Give thy thoughts no tongue," says Polonius,
"Nor any unproportioned thought his act"
(<u>Ham</u>. 1.3.59-60).

[The parentheses contain the act, scene, and line numbers, separated by periods. When included in parenthetical references, titles of the books of the
Bible and well-known literary works are often abbreviated—*Gen.* for *Genesis* and *Ado* for *Much Ado about Nothing,* for example.]

"I muse my life-long hate, and without flinch / I
bear it nobly as I live my part," says Claude McKay
in his bitterly ironic poem "The White City" (3-4).

[Notice that a slash [/] is used to separate lines of poetry run in with the
text. The parenthetical reference cites the lines quoted.]

The List of Works Cited

Parenthetical references refer to a **list of works cited** that includes all the
sources you refer to in your paper. (If your list includes all the works consulted, whether you cite them or not, use the title *Works Consulted.*) Begin
the works cited list on a new page, continuing the page numbers of the paper. For example, if the text of the paper ends on page six, the works cited
section will begin on page seven.

Center the title *Works Cited* one inch from the top of the page. Arrange entries alphabetically, according to the last name of each author (or the first word of the title if the author is unknown). Articles—*a, an,* and *the*—at the beginning of a title are not considered first words. Thus, *A Handbook of Critical Approaches to Literature* would be alphabetized under *H.* In order to conserve space, publishers' names are abbreviated—for example, *Harcourt* for Harcourt Brace College Publishers. Double-space the entire works cited list between and within entries. Begin typing each entry at the left margin, and indent subsequent lines five spaces or one-half inch. The entry itself generally has three divisions—author, title, and publishing information—separated by periods.*

A book by a single author

> Kingston, Maxine Hong. <u>The Woman Warrior: Memoirs of a Girlhood among Ghosts</u>. New York: Knopf, 1976.

A book by two or three authors

> Feldman, Burton, and Robert D. Richardson. <u>The Rise of Modern Mythology</u>. Bloomington: Indiana UP, 1972.

[Notice that only the *first* author's name is in reverse order.]

A book by more than three authors

> Guerin, Wilfred, et al., eds. <u>A Handbook of Critical Approaches to Literature</u>. 3rd. ed. New York: Harper, 1992.

[Instead of using *et al.,* you may list all the authors' names in the order in which they appear on the title page.]

Two or more works by the same author

> Novoa, Juan-Bruce. <u>Chicano Authors: Inquiry by Interview</u>, Austin: U of Texas P, 1980.

---

*The fourth edition of the *MLA Handbook for Writers of Research Papers* (1995) shows a single space after all end punctuation.

      ---. "Themes in Rudolfo Anaya's Work." Address
         given at New Mexico State University, Las
         Cruces. 11 Apr. 1987.

[List two or more works by the same author in alphabetical order by title. Include the author's full name in the first entry; use three unspaced hyphens followed by a period to take the place of the author's name in second and subsequent entries.]

An edited book

      Oosthuizen, Ann, ed. <u>Sometimes When It Rains: Writ-</u>
         <u>ings by South African Women</u>. New York: Pandora,
         1987.

[Note that the abbreviation *ed.* stands for *editor.*]

A book with a volume number

      Eagleton, T. Allston. <u>A History of the New York</u>
         <u>Stage</u>. Vol. 2. Englewood Cliffs: Prentice.
         1987.

[All three volumes have the same title.]

      Durant, Will, and Ariel Durant. <u>The Age of Napoleon:</u>
         <u>A History of European Civilization from 1789 to</u>
         <u>1815</u>. New York: Simon, 1975.

[Each volume has a different title, so you may cite an individual book without referring to the other volumes.]

A short story, poem, or play in a collection of the author's work

      Gordimer, Nadine. "Once upon a Time." <u>"Jump" and</u>
         <u>Other Stories</u>. New York: Farrar, 1991. 23-30.

A short story in an anthology

      Salinas, Marta. "The Scholarship Jacket." <u>Nosotros:</u>
         <u>Latina Literature Today</u>. Ed. Maria del Carmen

Boza, Beverly Silva, and Carmen Valle. Bingham-
ton: Bilingual, 1986. 68-70.

[The inclusive page numbers follow the year of publication. Note that here
the abbreviation *Ed.* stands for *Edited by.*]

A poem in an anthology

Simmerman, Jim. "Child's Grave, Hale County, Ala-
bama." The Pushcart Prize, X: Best of the Small
Presses. Ed. Bill Henderson. New York: Penguin,
1986. 198-99.

A play in an anthology

Hughes, Langston. Mother and Child. Black Drama Anthology. Ed. Woodie King and Ron Miller. New
York: NAL, 1986.399-406.

An article in an anthology

Forster, E. M. "Flat and Round Characters." The Theory of the Novel. Ed. Philip Stevick. New York:
Free, 1980. 223-31.

More than one selection from the same anthology

If you are using more than one selection from an anthology, cite the anthology in one entry. In addition, list each individual selection separately, including the author and title of the selection, the anthology editor's last
name, and the inclusive page numbers.

Kirszner, Laurie G., and Stephen R. Mandell, eds.
Literature: Reading, Reacting, Writing. 3rd ed.
Fort Worth: Harcourt, 1997.
Rich, Adrienne. "Diving into the Wreck." Kirszner
and Mandell 874-76.

A translation

Carpentier, Alejo. Reasons of State. Trans. Francis
Partridge. New York: Norton, 1976.

An article in a journal with continuous pagination in each issue

LeGuin, Ursula K. "American Science Fiction and the
    Other." <u>Science Fiction Studies</u> 2 (1975):
    208-10.

An article with separate pagination in each issue

Grossman, Robert. "The Grotesque in Faulkner's
    'A Rose for Emily.'" <u>Mosaic</u> 20.3 (1987): 40-55.

[20.3 signifies volume 20, issue 3.]

An article in a magazine

Milosz, Czeslaw. "A Lecture." <u>New Yorker</u> 22 June
    1992: 32.
"Solzhenitsyn: An Artist Becomes an Exile." <u>Time</u>
    25 Feb. 1974: 34+.

[34+ indicates that the article appears on pages that are not consecutive; in
this case the article begins on page 34 and then continues on page 37. An
article with no listed author is entered by title on the works cited list.]

An article in a daily newspaper

Oates, Joyce Carol. "When Characters from the Page
    Are Made Flesh on the Screen." <u>New York Times</u>
    23 Mar. 1986, late ed.: C1+.

[C1+ indicates that the article begins on page 1 of Section C and continues
on a subsequent page.]

An article in a reference book

"Dance Theatre of Harlem." <u>The New Encyclopaedia
    Britannica: Micropaedia</u>. 15th ed. 1987.

[You do not need to include publication information for well-known reference books.]

Grimstead, David. "Fuller, Margaret Sarah." <u>Encyclo-
    pedia of American Biography</u>. Ed. John A. Gar-
    raty. New York: Harper, 1974.

[You must include publication information when citing reference books that are not well known.]

A CD-ROM: Entry with a print version

> Zurbach, Kate. "The Linguistic Roots of Three
>   Terms." <u>Linguistic Quarterly</u> 37 (1994): 12–47.
>   <u>Infotrac: Magazine Index Plus</u>. CD-ROM. Informa-
>   tion Access. Jan. 1996.

[When you cite information with a print version from a CD-ROM, include the publication information, the underlined title of the database (<u>Infotrac: Magazine Index Plus</u>), the publication medium (CD-ROM), the name of the company that produced the CD-ROM (Information Access), and the electronic publication date.]

A CD-ROM: Entry with no print version

> "Surrealism." <u>Encarta 1996</u>. CD-ROM. Redmond: Micro-
>   soft, 1996.

[If you are citing a part of a work, include the title in quotation marks.]

> <u>A Music Lover's Multimedia Guide to Beethoven's 5th</u>.
>   CD-ROM. Spring Valley: Interactive, 1993.

[If you are citing an entire work, include the underlined title.]

An online source: Entry with a print version

> Dekoven, Marianne. "Utopias Limited: Post-sixties
>   and Postmodern American Fiction." <u>Modern Fic-
>   tion Studies</u> 41.1 (Spring 1995): 121–34.
>   17 Mar. 1996 <http://muse.jhu.edu/journals/
>   MFS/v041/41.1 dekoven.html>.

[When you cite information with a print version from an online source, include the publication information for the printed source, the number of pages or the number of paragraphs (if available), and the date of access. Include the electronic address, or URL, in angle brackets. Information from a commercial computer service—America Online, Prodigy, and CompuServ, for example—will not have an electronic address.]

```
O'Hara, Sandra. "Reexamining the Canon." Time 13 May
     1994: 27. America Online. 22 Aug. 1994.
```

An online source: Entry with no print version

```
"Romanticism." Academic American Encyclopedia. Sept.
     1996. Prodigy. 6 Nov. 1995.
```

[This entry shows that the material was accessed on November 6, 1996.]

An online source: Public Posting

```
Peters, Olaf. "Studying English through German."
     Online posting. 29 Feb. 1996. Foreign Language
     Forum, Multi Language Section. CompuServe.
     15 Mar. 1996.
Gilford, Mary. "Dog Heroes in Children's Litera-
     ture." 4 Oct. 1996. Newsgroup alt.animals.dogs.
     America Online. 23 Mar. 1996.
```

[**WARNING:** Using information from online forums and newsgroups is risky. Contributors are not necessarily experts, and frequently they are incorrect and misinformed. Unless you can be certain that the information you are receiving from these sources is reliable, do not use it in your papers.]

An online source: Electronic Text

```
Twain, Mark. The Adventures of Huckleberry Finn.
     From The Writing of Mark Twain. Vol. 13.
     New York: Harper, 1970. Wiretap.spies.
     13 Jan. 1996 <http.//www.sci.dixie.edu/
     DixieCollege/Ebooks/huckfin.html>.
```

[This electronic text was originally published by Harper. The name of the repository for the electronic edition is Wiretap.spies. (underlined)]

An online source: E-Mail

```
Adkins, Camille. E-Mail to the author. 8 June 1995.
```

An interview

> Brooks, Gwendolyn. "Interviews." <u>Triquarterly</u> 60
>   (1984): 405-10.

A lecture or address

> Novoa, Juan-Bruce. "Themes in Rudolfo Anaya's Work."
>   New Mexico State University, Las Cruces,
>   11 Apr. 1987.

A film or videocassette

> "<u>A Worn Path</u>." By Eudora Welty. Dir. John Reid and
>   Claudia Velasco. Perf. Cora Lee Day and Con-
>   chita Ferrell. Videocassette. Harcourt, 1994.

[In addition to the title, the director, and the year, include other pertinent information such as the principal performers.]

Explanatory Notes

Explanatory notes, indicated by a superscript (a raised number) in the text, may be used to cite several sources at once or to provide commentary or explanations that do not fit smoothly into your paper. The full text of these notes appears on the first numbered page following the last page of the paper. (If your paper has no explanatory notes, the works cited page follows the last page of the paper.) Like works cited entries, explanatory notes are double-spaced within and between entries. However, the first line of each explanatory note is indented five spaces (or one-half inch), with subsequent lines flush with the left-hand margin.

To Cite Several Sources

In the paper

> Surprising as it may seem, there have been many
> attempts to define literature.[1]

In the note

[1] For an overview of critical opinion, see Arnold 72; Eagleton 1–2; Howe 43–44; and Abrams 232–34.

TO PROVIDE EXPLANATIONS

In the paper

In recent years Gothic novels have achieved great popularity.[3]

In the note

[3] Gothic novels, works written in imitation of medieval romances, originally relied on supernatural occurrences. They flourished in the late eighteenth and early nineteenth centuries.

Credits